School Organisation

S. E. Bray

BIBLIOLIFE

SCHOOL ORGANISATION

BY

S. E. BRAY, M.A.,

RESPONDENT OF TRINITY COLLEGE, DUBLIN; BARRISTER-AT-LAW;
INSPECTOR OF SCHOOLS TO THE LONDON COUNTY COUNCIL; AUTHOR OF
"BRITANNIA'S REALM," PART-AUTHOR OF "AFRICA," ETC.

LONDON: W. B. CLIVE,

University Tutorial Press Ld.

(*University Correspondence College Press*),

157 DRURY LANE, W.C.
1905.

PREFACE.

This small volume is primarily intended for students in training preparing for the Final or Certificate Examination It does not, therefore, claim to be an exhaustive treatise on School Organisation but, as the treatment of the subject is mainly empirical, and the information is drawn from a variety of English and foreign sources, the writer expresses the hope that the book will be found useful to the practical teacher.

Acknowledgments of indebtedness have been made, in most instances, by means of footnotes in the various pages The volumes thus indicated will amply repay perusal

The subject-matter of Chapter VI is more fully dealt with from the hygienic point of view in *Certificate School Hygiene*, published in the same series as the present work

The writer's thanks are due to his colleague, Mr. J Nickal, for helpful guidance

CONTENTS.

CHAPTER I.

CHAPTER II.

The School and the School Department.

CHAPTER III

Organisation in connection with District Adminis-tration.

CHAPTER IV

DISCIPLINE

CHAPTER V

SCHOOL RECORDS AND REGISTRATION

CHAPTER VI

THE SCHOOL PREMISES IN CONNECTION WITH ORGANISATION.

SCHOOL ORGANISATION.

INTRODUCTORY

"The problem of education is the eternal problem of human nature "—MAZZINI.

" Let us grant that as for every other art, there is also a technique for Pedagogics which can be learned only in a practical way "— WAITZ

To establish clearly the meaning of the term Organisation, it is desirable to go back etymologically to the original Greek —the tool or instrument[1] with which work[2] is performed Applied biologically, *organ* designates a part performing a given physiological function. Again, as the life of an individual is, in a physiological sense, the sum of its functions, so the aggregate of its organs is called an *organism* Finally, an artificial organism, in which a variety of members and instruments are disposed in order to secure a desired end, is termed *organisation* As often happens, the same abstract term signifies both an *act* and an *effect*, or an act and a state—so in this case organisation covers both the *arranging* and the *arrangement* The application of this word pedagogically is a wide one. The co-ordination of the schools of a county, town, or

[1] ὄργανον (Latin, *organum*) = tool or instrument
[2] ἔργον = work

district; the division of a school into various departments; the working plans laid down by a head teacher for the effective teaching and proper governance of his scholars—all these come legitimately within the meaning of school organisation.

It is, however, the last-named phase of organisation that will be principally considered in these pages—the foundations upon which instruction and discipline may and do rest.

The working plans must necessarily be influenced by the character of the building, especially by the number, size and distribution of the class-rooms ; by the number and quality of the staff : by the age and attainments of the scholars ; by the subjects of instruction and the methods by which they are taught ; by the character of the discipline ; and, lastly, by the specific aim which the organiser has in view.

The nucleus of school organisation is sound classification. The fitting of the teacher to the class, the adjustment of the class to the room, the adaptation of the subjects and methods to the scholars, the proper distribution of time, etc, are the additions that assist in making a coherent and unified whole.

The true basis for educational theory is the individual; but the application of this theory is almost invariably collective—that is, adapted as far as practicable to groups of scholars approximately possessing equal attainments, but necessarily varying in ability and character.

It is manifest that the best organisation is that which, *cœteris paribus*, will produce the maximum of educational effect in a given time. One of the conditions precedent to sound organisation is clear and distinct educational aim. The end of education is not the theme of this volume, but as bearing on organisation and especially on choice of studies, some remarks are permissible. It is considered that the dominant characteristic of this aim should be purely ethical, that it should point to moral training, not by mere words, but through the heart and imagination, through example, through forces that are part of the energies of a child's nature and enter into the very essence of its soul In the words of Ruskin, let the children get their "breastplate of truth first and every earthly stone will shine in it." A fine character will satisfy all the theories as to the ends of life a mere intellectual prodigy will satisfy none.

The intellectual faculty must, of course, secure its due share of attention. Its development naturally occupies the major portion of time devoted to school life. Mental alertness must be encouraged, reasoning power must be trained, and an intelligent curiosity developed. It is well, too, for the theory of to-day to become the practice of to-morrow "The value of knowledge culminates in its use." [1]

Physical culture must also have its claims recognised Rousseau's ideal on this point is a beautiful one, viz, that all parts of the human body, when in motion, should harmonise with each other, like the sounds of a musical chord.

As the school is State-aided and guided by State regulations, and as, too, it is a unit in State organisation, so in a democratic country it must be in touch with public sentiment and be limited by the public purse. Hence a multitude of forces converge upon the school, and streams of influence surround it. If, therefore, the teacher is not always able to organise on what he considers to be the best lines, he ought not to allow his educational faith to be weakened nor his ideals to lose their guiding power;

[1] De Garmo,

for there is still an immense field for the play of
personality and the operation of initiative, both within
and beyond the school premises No school is bounded
by its four walls Discipline in its best form calls for
teachers who are students of the endless problem of
human nature, and bids those associated with the training
of infants especially to remember that young children
spend most of their lives in fairyland

As a nation finds it necessary, from time to time, to
add to its laws and to repeal others, so it is necessary for
a school, if it is to preserve its health and vitality, to be
sometimes throwing off or modifying old practices and
adding new ones Change is a law of nature Change
must also, in a modified sense, be part of the practice of a
school. It is impossible for any institution to thrive
permanently unless new ideas are occasionally given play
in its constitution New conditions must arise with the
advance of time Stagnation is death *Non progredi est
regredi* Conformity to the law of progress is imperative.

Change, however, must not be introduced for the sake
of change When introduced it should be like the change
of an organic body, " not that of a cloud " Before anything is discarded or anything added, mature consideration
should lead to it

The assistant teacher's interest in the school ought not
to be limited to his class. His horizon, theoretically
at least, should be as wide and extended as that of his
chief. Everything that concerns the school as a whole
should excite his interest and bring his help if desired
Loyal co-operation with the head teacher and devotion to
his scholars are the sum of his duties.

On the other hand, the wise head teacher extends a
tactful consideration to each member of the staff, and
remembers that all are not to be influenced and directed

by the same means. He bears in mind, too, that it is mainly through the agency of the class teachers that each individual is reached, and the law of the school upheld

The empirical character of much of the following dissertation will be manifest. In many respects when dealing with the social sciences, and in pedagogy, perhaps, no less than any other, experience is the only guide The variety of circumstances that must be considered, the variation of character, and the difference of local aims, are so great as to render a purely scientific treatment an impossibility However, a good school mostly possesses the same essential features wherever found. " It always nourishes the same interests; it always leads to thinking as well as observation ; it always points to the beautiful in the world and to the sublime above it, it always awakens sympathetic participation for domestic and civil weal and woe "[1]

This quotation indicates the character of the work to be accomplished It is clear that a sound organised basis is essential Personal enthusiasm, an insight into child nature, a knowledge of the procedure adopted by the best educationists and of the principles underlying this procedure will probably be the teacher's most suitable outfit

[1] Herbart

CHAPTER I.

THE CLASS.

The Class as Unit.

ALTHOUGH the individual is the unit in a school, yet in the sense of organisation the class must be taken as the real unit, that is, an aggregate of individuals grouped together for purposes of a definite course of instruction.

It is manifest that a lecturer engaged in the elucidation of any subject is in a very different position to that of the class teacher. In the former case, the number of people who constitute the audience is immaterial provided the speaker's voice is able to reach every person in the assembly. It is no part of the lecturer's duty to see that his audience *has* profited by his expositions; nor to apply tests to discover how far each person has acquired the information he desired to convey. The mere lecturer's duties end with his best efforts to interest or instruct his audience. The teacher's task is much more far-reaching than this. He has not only to expound, unfold and interest, not only to see that everything is presented in such a way as to cultivate each child's moral and intellectual faculties, but also to see that the information given goes home, as far as possible, to every member of the class. In other words, more generally stated, he must apply David Stow's maxim, "The teacher has not taught unless the child has learned."

To accomplish this, the varying needs of each scholar, even the one with the least mental power, must be carefully considered As the speed of a fleet has to be governed by the slowest vessel comprised in it, so the rate of progress of a class must, to some extent, be influenced by its dullest member. There is nothing detrimental in this so far as mere curriculum is concerned It is only nature's way of suggesting the brake *Go slowly and be thorough* is the best possible motto for the class teacher Testing, revision, supplementing are the necessary accompaniments to substantial class progress Moral control must be inculcated[1] and moral stimulus applied. From all this it will be seen how essential it is to place strict limitations on the size of the class if the teacher's work is to be wholly and individually effective.

Size of Classes and Variations.

These limitations, however, will vary with circumstances, even supposing that the standard of efficiency is constant It is clear that the size of a class may depend upon the ability of the teacher—the ease and lucidity or otherwise with which he is able to present facts, his moral power, his insight into character, his energy, the intensity and extent of his capability of covering the class with his eyes; it will vary as the scholars' attainments and receptive powers are more or less on a level; it may vary according to the character of the subject of instruction and the way in which it is taught. A practical science lesson, for example, with only one teacher in charge,

[1] "The worth of man depends not upon his knowledge but upon his will."—HERBART

should not, as a rule, be given to more than twenty
scholars   A vocal music lesson, on the other hand, might
desirably include as many pupils as a hall or room would
accommodate, provided the instructor is capable of holding and interesting them

The size of a class may, and does often, vary according
to its relative position in the school—whether it is one of
the upper or lower classes. In the upper school, the
necessity for revision, correction of exercises, and general
closer supervision of the work, makes large classes a
practical impossibility if any high standard of attainment is aimed at. And finally the number of scholars in
a class must vary according to the Regulations of the
Board of Education and those (if any) of the Local
Authority, so far as they concern the accommodation[1] of
the room or the status[2] of the class teacher

There remains, however, one more condition of variation
to be noticed which is an exception to one cited above. It
is evident that children of extremely low attainments and
of exceptionally poor ability should be grouped together
in much smaller classes than those possessing normal
powers of progress.

The limitations to the size of the class, in the past, have
been extremely varied. They have been determined in most
instances, more by the iron hand of economy than by
educational considerations Of late years, however, some
enlightened Local Authorities have done much to reduce
the class to reasonable limits, with the indirect result that
this influence has reacted upon others and produced a
general tendency in the right direction In 1874 the
average number of children to one teacher in the country
schools of Brunswick was 88. The English limit for a

[1] Art. 14 and Art. 19, Code 1904   [2] Art. 12 and Art. 32, Code 1904.

certificated class teacher works out at 69 children in
" habitual attendance."[1] Similarly an uncertificated teacher
is limited to 52 and a pupil teacher to 34 on this basis.

It is almost axiomatic to say that these numbers are too
large, bearing in mind the searchingly individualistic
duties that devolve upon the class teacher. They are faulty
in three respects. In the first place, the numbers are too
high absolutely, in the second place, no allowance is made
for classes of scholars containing two or more grades or
standards; and thirdly, no differentiation is admitted
between the upper and lower classes of a school. The last
two points are very important. No staffing scheme can be
considered satisfactory which excludes these from view,
unless it is an exceedingly liberal one based on general
principles.

Some modification of the official rule seems to be
desirable.[2] The warning attached to the article in question
appears to indicate an impending change. It must be
understood that the Board of Education only lays down
the *minimum* staff as " a condition precedent to a grant."
This minimum " must not be understood to indicate that a
school thus staffed is necessarily efficient. In every case
the circumstances of the individual school will be considered in relation to the educational conditions of the
area and the sufficiency of the staff thus tested."

In Hungary the law does not allow more than 80 pupils

[1] " Habitual attendance " is not equivalent to average attendance
[see Art 11, Code 1904, and compare with Art 12 (*a*)]. The averages
would, of course, be less. The average for the London County Council
schools including head teachers is 41-42. In these schools the limit
for a certificated assistant teacher is about 50 in average attendance.
This is based on an unwritten law which is often generously inter-
preted. Pupil teachers are not as a rule considered in the staffing
arrangements, for they only attend school half-time.

[2] Art 12 (*a*), Code 1904.

for one teacher. In the schools, however, classes may be
seen of 40 and under, but most of the classes are far too
large. In the Netherlands a scale of staffing is adopted
on the basis of accommodation. The number of pupils
per class teacher works out at about 50. In Sweden in
1898 the number per teacher was 47.[1]

In the United States and the Colonies the practice
compares favourably with ours. In New York the limit
for a class is 50 and the average attendance per teacher
is 39,[2] excluding the head and visiting teachers. In
Queensland the average for a teacher is 29.[3]

The class numbers vary greatly in different parts of
Germany. The tabulated statement below represents the
average number per teacher in the Berlin schools,[4] Class I
being the highest and corresponding with Standard Ex.
VII. in England.

Class	I	35.	Class	V.	50.
„	II.	35.	„	VI.	54.
„	III.	41.	„	VII.	56.
„	IV.	45.	„	VIII.	57.

In Berlin the schools are organised on the "eight-class"
system, the scholars varying in age from 6 to 14. The
classes represent grades similar to the English standards,
now not officially recognised.

Assuming that the Berlin numbers do not differ materially from the roll, they may be regarded as a reasonable

[1] See Special Reports.

[2] The average roll per teacher, including the head, is 44. *Vide*
Report of City Superintendent for 1903.

[3] Report for 1903.

[4] Report of Mr. Andrew, Scotch Education Department, 1901. The
average number of pupils per teacher for the German Empire was 61
in 1901. *Vide* "History and Organisation of Public Education in
the German Empire, 1904," by Dr. Lexis.

compromise between economical and educational claims, and present on the whole a satisfactory working arrangement For English conditions, however, especially in some areas, the numbers in the three lowest classes must be considered too high for thoroughly efficient work Something approaching the educational ideal will be attained when the average number of scholars per teacher in a department is not allowed to exceed 40[1] but as economical considerations have necessarily to play an important part in education as in all other mundane things, it will probably be a long time before this desirable limit is reached. It is no more practicable to disregard these considerations than it is "to leap the world to come."

Reference has been already made to the accommodation of rooms and the status of the teacher as two of the factors in determining the size of classes, the Code very properly forbidding overcrowding and overweighting. It is impracticable here to deal with all the peculiarities of this case The one instance may be taken in which a class is too large for the status[2] of the teacher, but not too large for the room. The organiser then has two courses open to him—either to make a suitable selection from the pupils covering the excess and draft them to another class, or to give the teacher such supplemental aid as will satisfy the Code

The New York regulation deals with this and similar cases, if otherwise incurable, by transferring the excess scholars to another school. Another method of dealing with these constantly recurring difficulties and especially that phase of them which concerns the highest classes in a

---

[1] The Dutch teachers of the Social Democratic Federation are aiming to limit each class to 24 pupils. (*Schoolmaster*, Sept. 10, 1904.)

[2] Art. 12 (*a*), Code 1904.

school, which are often too large at the beginning of the educational year and too small towards the close of it, is to consider each room as having a marginal accommodation, that is, both a maximum and a minimum accommodation, the maximum only to be recognised as a temporary arrangement. Of course the laws of health would have to be considered in connexion with this proposal, and the maximum would have to be based on healthy conditions, whilst the accommodation of the department would remain an invariable quantity founded on the total of the minimum accommodation[1] of each room in it. Probably the most convenient marginal accommodation would be one in the ratio of four to five, or one additional place for every four on the minimum basis.

As there is no necessary connexion between the number of pupils in a class or grade and the accommodation of a room or the status of a teacher, ever-recurring difficulties will arise which the organiser must face and overcome as best he can. Even the official limit of the teaching power assigned to a teacher is not always a safe guide. The personal equation must be considered too. Of these three elements in organisation, the organiser is powerless over two, except in so far as he may have a choice of assistants of varied status and power. He must of course take the line of least resistance and make the class fit the teacher, and, as far as practicable, the room. It is essential that he should fit the teacher. But even when this has been done at the commencement of the educational year, the organiser's troubles are not ended in this direction. Fresh admissions will come as a disturbing factor, especially in the lower classes, and the uneven progress of the upper groups of children in the various classes will tax his

[1] This would prevent overcrowding. The proposal is only intended to meet the temporary needs of a class here and there.

resources, supposing he wishes to promote pupils on their merits before the close of the year.

The annual courses of instruction known as the standards have been valuable on account of their well-known character, their general acceptance and application; but being annual, it has been too often assumed that promotions ought not to be made until the end of the year, when, as nearly as practicable, equality of attainments could still form the basis for a new organisation. The past rigidity of the standards, coupled with their annual character, has, no doubt, been partially responsible for the unnecessary retardation of many scholars and the want of more rapid progress of children above the average in ability. Now that standardisation has been officially dropped, except for certificates of proficiency, probably it will be conceded that there are no cardinal virtues in the calendar or educational year. The organiser can now, though a great deal of freedom has previously been given by the Code, so arrange his courses of instruction as to meet the special needs of his pupils, and make them as pliable and as adaptable to varying circumstances as possible. It is not necessary under existing regulations that the courses should correspond from year to year, provided reasonable grounds can be shown for fresh or even radical departures. No wise teacher, however, would attempt any great change such as would seriously interfere with the due correlation of studies.

What has been said concerning the standards equally applies to the steps or grades in the infant school, but this matter will be considered later when the subject of promotion is discussed.

Large Classes.

It must not be supposed that large classes are only to be regarded as an unmixed evil That such classes leave much to be desired is incontestable but they have some weighty advantages Sympathy is a potent educational force. Sympathy of numbers, springing from each unit in a mass which works with the same aim and in which each is bound to the other by ties of class fellowship, makes for friendly rivalry, moral strength, and intellectual zest. The larger the class, within certain limits, the greater is the play of competing forces. The rousing of moral power sharpens the intellectual appetite

Large classes, too, tend to encourage and develop individual reliance and resource If there is a real danger connected with recent educational developments, it is that too much is being done for the scholars by the teacher The essence of education lies in the *scholars'* doing, not the teacher's Froebel's motto applies to the pupil, not to the teacher The latter's true function is that of guide, philosopher and friend—not a guide who always leads and shows the way, except by moral example, but a guide who will help the pupil to find the right path chiefly by exciting his reasoning power.

The sympathy arising from numbers acts on the teacher as well as on the scholars That peculiar unifying moral tie that holds an able teacher to his class is alive with emotional currents passing from him to the pupils and from the pupils to him, with mutual advantage. They give the teacher an added power, and often enable him to transcend himself

But all this presupposes a strong teacher It must not be taken as a pæan of praise to large classes It is merely an attempt to show the sturdy side of a weak position. The advocacy for a class of forty pupils stands for all

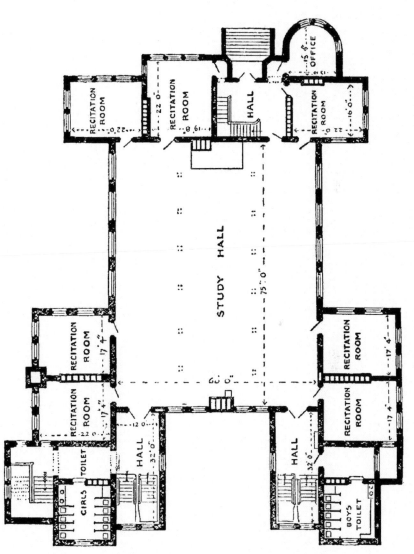

PLAN OF AN AMERICAN SCHOOL, SHOWING STUDY HALL AND
RECITATION ROOMS.

ordinary purposes. There are, however, cases and
occasions when large classes are desirable or admissible.
A vocal music class, for example, might be often the
better for combining two or more classes, the only necessary limitations being physical considerations and the
teacher's ability to control and instruct. Lantern lessons
also lend themselves to bigger classes than are admissible
under ordinary conditions. The preparation class is
another example. This is a device practised in American
schools, by which the central hall is utilised for private
study. This is done to encourage resource and independent effort. It also economises staff, for the
teachers thus employed in supervision are only qualified
to take a smaller number of pupils under ordinary class
conditions. The recital lessons take place in the adjoining
rooms, as seen in the accompanying plan. This is, however, only practicable in buildings specially adapted to the
purpose.

The One-Class School.

This kind of school is usually found in thinly populated
and isolated districts, the teacher being unaided except,
perhaps, for needlework. The one teacher, therefore, constitutes both the head and assistant staff. Monitors,
however, are usually employed. Organisation, under such
circumstances, might appear to reach its vanishing point:
but in reality it ought to find, in a limited way, its highest
development, if sound efficiency is to be secured and
maintained.

The teacher has practically to solve the problem of being
corporeally in two or more places at the same time, and
also to impregnate the atmosphere of the school with his
spiritual presence. The difficulties of the position are

apparent, especially if, as sometimes happens, the *one* class—which is, by the way, a misnomer—consists of pupils ranging in progress from Standard I to VI or VII, and occasionally otherwise complicated by the presence of infants when the sole teacher is a woman. Under conditions like these the mutual help or monitorial system becomes imperative, much as its use must be deprecated

The question of the unification of such small schools into a central one, or their absorption into existing larger and neighbouring centres, has been successfully dealt with in some countries. Reasonable distance must, of course, be a factor in any satisfactory solution of the difficulty, even when the distance is covered by vehicles. In America this plan is extensively practised. Canada, too, has recognised its utility, and is developing the same system.

In this country,[1] Devon, Cornwall, and Gloucestershire bring children of scattered districts to school in this way. The attractions of a ride, combined with protection from rain and other inclemencies of the weather, have brought about a better attendance whilst the advantages of instruction in a large school, meeting in a healthy, commodious building, possessing a stimulating *esprit de corps*, and permitting an organisation on a basis of sound classification, are too evident to be named.

Assuming, however, that no such desirable conveniences exist, it is extremely difficult, if not impossible, to suggest a satisfactory classification and distribution of teaching power for small schools of this type, especially as they vary considerably in different localities. Probably the best organisation would be secured by the teacher taking full advantage of the latitude allowed by the Code in the

---

[1] See Art. by J. C. Medd in *School*, ii., 88.

way of classification. History, geography, grammar, etc,
should be taught in not more than three sections, and, as
far as possible, subjects that lend themselves to individual
and private effort should intervene between each oral
lesson. The essential thing is for the teacher to regard
the lessons on the "class subjects" as one of the chief
means of reaching each pupil in the matter of moral and
intellectual training

In the rural schools of north-west France the average
number of pupils in a school with a single unaided teacher
is about forty. Some such schools, however, have higher
numbers. The law allows an additional teacher when
the number of pupils exceeds fifty [1]

The Class as Unit in a Department.

If a department is to advance as a whole, unity of
educational aim must find its expression in each class.
Consistent method everywhere is essential to due progress
The teacher should be attached to that class in which his
fullest powers are likely to be displayed. It is not only
mere teaching ability that has to be weighed in this connection, but also moral disciplinary power and grasp of
knowledge. In other words, the teacher should fit the
class and the class the teacher

First, the teacher must fit the class in the official sense,
that is, as understood by the Board of Education [2]   He
should also fit the class in the sense of aptitude. It often
happens that these two by no means correspond. Officially,
a class numbering about sixty scholars is suitable for a
certificated teacher   There is no doubt that this number
is too high, under ordinary conditions, for efficient work.

[1] See "Rural Schools of N.W France." Special Reports Vol 7.
[2] Art 12 (a), Code 1904.

TIME TABLE OF A ONE CLASS MIXED NATIONAL SCHOOL IN THE SOUTH OF ENGLAND

STANDARD	9.0 to 9.10	9.10 to 9.40	9.40 to 9.45	9.45 to 10.35	10.35 to 10.50	10.50 to 11.25	11.25 to 12.0		1.15 to 1.20	1.20 to 1.55	1.55 to 2.35	2.35 to 2.45	2.45 to 3.25	3.25 to 3.30
III to VI / I and II	Assemble, Prayers, and Registers marked	Religious Instruction	Registers closed	Arith. / "	Recreation	Dict or Trans / Reading	Reading (Hist) Dict. or Trans.	Mon.	Assemble and mark and close Registers	Geography Elementary Science	Singing	Recreation	Copy Book / "	Prayers and Dismissal
III to VI / I and II				Arith. / "		Composition / Reading	Reading / Composition	Tues.		B Spelling, Drawing G. Needlework / B Spelling, Drawing G. Needlework	Spelling, Drawing, Needlework		Recitation Elementary Science	
III to VI / I and II				Arith. / "		Grammar / Reading	Reading (Geo) Dict or Trans	Wed.		Geography Elementary Science	Singing / "		Copy Books / *	
III to VI / I and II				Arith. / "		Composition / Reading	Reading (Hist) Grammar	Thurs.		B Arith. Drawing G. Needlework / B Arith. Drawing G. Needlework	Arith. Drawing Needlework		Geography Recitation	
III to VI / I and II				Arith. / "		Dict or Trans / Reading	Reading / Composition	Fri.		B Spelling, Drawing G. Needlework / B Spelling, Drawing G. Needlework	Spelling, Drawing, Needlework		Optional Lesson	

19

ANALYSIS OF TIME TABLE

Religious Instruction and Devotional Ex.	3 hrs. 0 mins		Object Lessons	1 hr 45 mins
Reading	2 " 55 "		Singing	1 " 0 "
Writing, Copy Books	1 " 10 "		Drill	0 " 20 "
Dictation or Translation	1 " 10 "		Geography	1 " 45 "
Composition	1 " 10 "		History	1 " 10 "
Spelling	1 hr 10 mins			
Arithmetic	3 " 20 "			
Mental Arithmetic	0 " 50 "			
Recitation	0 " 35 "			
Needlework	3 " 45 "			
Drawing	2 " 15 "			

* Drill for 20 minutes   The teacher has no help except in Needlework. He supervises one section, while teaching the other.

It is especially too high for the upper classes, for the lowest class, and also in cases in which two or more grades of scholars are grouped to form one class   But the Board of Education regulation does not differentiate in this way, probably because it is exceedingly difficult to make rules that will equally well apply to various, and sometimes varying, local circumstances   Generally speaking, however, fifty scholars when there are two grades or standards together, and forty when there are three, should be regarded as the maximum number for one certificated teacher   H M Inspectors usually give a generous interpretation to the regulation in question

It almost invariably happens that a class has several pupils in excess or short of the number that can be allotted to a teacher   In case of excess, it is necessary to draft the extra pupils to another class, or to give the teacher in question supplementary aid in the form of a pupil teacher, or an uncertificated assistant ; or, again, a sub-division could be formed for which a pupil teacher, or an uncertificated teacher, could be held responsible   This latter plan, especially when the pupil teacher is solely responsible, is undesirable, not only on educational grounds, but because it throws a specific burden on the head to be in continual touch with the sub-division for purposes of direction and supervision, and this is not always possible.

If, on the other hand, the deficiency in numbers is small, it can generally be neglected ; and if, again, the excess is small—one or two—it may be left out of consideration for natural adjustments will be sure to come, sooner or later, to the organiser's assistance.

The class being formed, other difficulties arise in the shape of admission of new pupils and varying rates of progress   New pupils ought not to be allowed to retard a class unless the number of admissions is abnormally large.

The thoughtful teacher will find the means of giving a few fresh scholars odds and ends of attention, which will in some measure compensate them for lost ground, without allowing the majority of the class to suffer. Admissions, however, are necessarily a slightly disturbing element, and the question arises whether it is not desirable to place some restrictions upon them, especially when they are due to caprice This is done in many secondary schools In Berlin and some parts of the United States admissions are only allowed twice a year. In the interests of migratory scholars themselves some restrictive rule is eminently desirable. One partial way of mitigating the evil appears to lie in the adoption of the same educational year for schools in a district The head teachers, too, with a recognised system of professional etiquette, might do much in the same direction.

The other disturbing element, viz., the varying rate of progress, is the more difficult to deal with, considering the class as a whole. The normal rate in elementary schools has generally been accepted to be the annual courses prescribed by the standards for scholars ranging between the ages of six and fourteen. It has been assumed that the average scholar could take these yearly steps, commencing with Standard I., at about six and a-half years, without undue pressure, and that those who fall behind would be counterbalanced in number by others above the average in ability, and therefore presumably capable of advancing more rapidly than the ordinary child This assumption is not consonant with facts so far as some great areas are concerned, for the number of scholars who fall behind greatly outnumber those whose advance is beyond that of the yearly steps. Of course, this raises a question not only of national, but universal interest It cannot, however, be considered here. Suffice it to say that what was regarded as a normal rate of progress has not been realised, and therefore it is as well to note that the limitations of the " normal rate " have not yet been fixed

Departures from the normal are inevitable Percentages on this point in one district will not necessarily correspond with those in another district, because operating causes might be vastly different The teacher, therefore, must not assume that what is possible in one county is equally possible in another Over pressure is, perhaps, more deadly than sluggish work Hence the means must not only be suited to the ends, but also to the individual and in this respect the class teacher has shallows and depths to sound which must tax all his judgment, patience, and energy if real success is to attend his efforts No faith ought to be placed in rules formed *a priori* in dealing with this question [1]

The head teacher must be prepared to find considerable divergence in the rate of progress of the scholars The class teacher will find it necessary to adapt his pace to the class as a whole, and to see that every child advances in conformity with his ability and aptitude

Promotion.

The class has necessarily to be remodelled once in twelve months, that is at the end of the educational year All or the great majority of the scholars are then promoted to a higher class A few perhaps have not advanced sufficiently to secure promotion In some schools it is found practic-

[1] In London Provided Schools for the year ended Lady Day, 1904, there were in boys', girls' and mixed departments 27 per cent. of the scholars in the normal stage, 7 per cent. above the normal, and about 65 per cent. below it These percentages are based on the assumption that every child commences the work of Standard I at six and a-half years.

able to promote at the end of each of the two or three
terms into which the educational year is divided Such
promotion is usually carried out on the basis of examination This, however, is not a necessity. Promotion could
be as efficiently brought about by the record of a term's
individual work, supplemented, if considered desirable, by
examination in one or more special subjects

Most elementary schools carry out their promotions
annually This apparently has been found to work well
It would, however, be a mistake to accept this practice as a
safe and proper guide for every elementary school Indeed,
it may be doubted whether, under the existing freedom of
classification allowed to teachers, it ought to be rigidly
applied to any school A judicious mixture of both yearly
and term promotions seems the best A clever child who
has reasonably well mastered the work of a class in six
months ought not to be compelled to repeat that work
ad nauseam to the end of the year The effect of retention
in the same class, under these circumstances, is mischievous
in the extreme ; for the child loses interest, the mainspring
of attention and industry, and discontent and tedium
result The effects produced by this means often cling to
a scholar for the rest of his school life.

The chief objections to term promotions are (1) interruption to a steady and continuous year's work of the class
teacher, (2) the doubtful advantage of promoting a child
into a class that has already completed about one-half of
the year's course, and (3) the dislike of the class teacher
to have the best pupils removed. These are of minor
importance compared with the deleterious influence on the
child who is not allowed to go forward when he is reasonably fit to do so. Of these three objections (1) is more
imaginary than real, (2) is apparently strong: but the
clever child is found in practice to be able to overtake his

average school-fellow without undue strain; (3) is admittedly disheartening to the teacher.

If the smartest children are promoted to a higher class, equally intelligent scholars are promoted from a lower class to take their place—assuming, of course, that term promotions are general for the school—and though these cannot have the same attainments, yet they will, by natural ability, ever prevent the class becoming dull; and the class teacher should remember that it is his first duty to serve the best interests of his scholars, and therefore should subordinate himself to that duty.

These remarks apply, with some slight modifications, to the ordinary retarded scholar. At the end of the educational year every child in a class should be promoted, unless there is overwhelming evidence to support retardation. Generally speaking, nothing in school life is so demoralising and so deadening to the faculties as retention of a scholar in the same class for two or more years. Interest almost vanishes, and self-respect and self-reliance become less and less acute, under such circumstances; and this position becomes all the more pronounced if the scholar is already old for his standard or class. " Hope deferred maketh the heart sick ' has just as keen an application for the child as the man. If, however, there should be strong reasons for retardation, then the scholar should be encouraged to improve by the prospect of promotion at the end of three or six more months.

As already stated, a judicious mixture of both yearly and term promotions appears to be the best. In order, however, to carry out this effectively, some changes in the courses of instruction seem to be necessary. The steps known as the standards are based upon a year's work for the ordinary child. The plan commonly adopted by the organiser is so to arrange the lessons that these steps or

courses can be completed in about eight or nine months,
the remaining period of the year being spent in traversing
the ground already covered, laying special stress on material
points, making additions and emendations, and generally
putting upon the whole work its finishing touches

In lieu of this plan, it is suggested that the educational
year be divided into two terms, each of six months' duration ;
and that the standard courses be divided into two parts in
the ratio of about 2 to 1, or, perhaps better still, 5 to 2,
the larger portion of the course being taken in the first
six months,[1] and the smaller during the second, together
with such essential parts of the first term course as would
make a reasonably graduated syllabus suited to the child
a little above the average in ability This arrangement,
it is thought, would meet the needs of the ordinary
scholar in the way of recapitulation, and would place the
child drafted at the close of the first six months into a
position nearly equal to the one possessed by the ordinary
scholar at the commencement of the educational year, so
far as a graduated syllabus is concerned

This would cure the defect, under some existing practices,
of promoting children at the end of six months to a class
that has already done two-thirds of the year's work, and is
at the point of commencing the other third The promoted
pupil has then to take up the course at a point in which
some knowledge of what has been taught in the first half
of the year is, if not essential, at least desirable to ensure
satisfactory progress

Even with the suggested two-term courses in operation,
it would still be necessary to make the great majority of
the promotions at the close of the educational year , but
the gain in being able fittingly to promote at an earlier

---

[1] It would be well to complete the Arithmetic course during the first
term.

period, even a small percentage of the scholars, would be very great indeed

Nothing said here is intended to encourage premature advancement of the child, which only leads to disastrous results in later life A scholar's school career ought to be one of happiness; and happiness is not consistent with either physical or mental strain Only those children should, therefore, be promoted earlier than usual who can, without undue exertion, keep pace with the work An ill-nourished child,[1] for example, although possessed of more than ordinary mental activity and power, ought rather to have its activities restrained than stimulated and precocious children generally need careful vigilance to see they do not overtax their strength. The *whole* child is put into the teacher's keeping

The Educational Commission of the City of Chicago[2] has recommended, *inter alia*, " That the course of study be so adjusted as readily to permit of at least semi-annual promotion from grade to grade "

Again, Section 247 of the Rules and Regulations of the Public Schools of the City of Boston reads "The regular promotion of pupils from grade to grade shall be made in September and February Promotion of individual pupils may be made at any time by the Principal of the district with the approval of the Supervisor in charge."

---

[1] The L C.C Provisional Code 1904 (Art 77) reads " In order to prevent dull and delicate children from being unduly pressed, it is desirable that the Managers should form a small Health Sub-Committee to watch the cases of such children throughout the year," etc.

[2] See Report 1900 " Grade " roughly corresponds to "standard "

Age and Classification

Something must be said as to the bearing of age on classification and promotion. As a rule moral and intellectual power in a child is directly proportional to age Age, therefore, ought to be a factor in classification and promotion, though it sometimes happens that a scholar of twelve years is duller than a child of seven

(1) *Backward Scholars*

Generally, children who are old for this class or standard have less ability than their fellows, assuming, of course, that a proper system of promotion has been in operation Such children, by constant association with others so much younger than themselves, tend to lose their self-respect, and become an obstacle to good discipline They show this in many ways : there is a lack of industry, of interest, of tone, and, on the positive side, a decided tendency to be mischievous and troublesome Everything, therefore, ought to be done to rouse them to a proper sense of personal responsibility, and this can probably be best effected by promoting them, within reasonable limits, to work in that class with which pupils of approximately equal ages are associated Although such children will not fit the class in attainments, yet it will be generally found that they will learn, and improve in other respects, at a comparatively greater rate than if associated with children much younger than themselves

This has been found in many instances to work well in practice ; and it has a special application in the case of those who are, say, within six months of leaving school altogether If they fail to be brought into teaching contact with one of the two highest classes in the school, their school life ends without even the sense, much less

the acquisition, of that fine tone and moral responsibility
that invariably characterise the two upper classes in any
really good educational establishment. Such a loss is
practically irreparable If, therefore, children of this
kind are not hopelessly remote, in attainments and mental
grasp, from the upper classes, it is eminently desirable
that they should be in close touch with those classes, if
only intermittently, in such occasional lessons as are given
in history, geography, Scripture, literature, and other
subjects that lend themselves to oral instruction

(2) *The Ungraded Class*

Another method of dealing with children who are old
for their standards is to have a special class for them—
an ungraded or remove class. This plan, however, will
generally be found impracticable in most buildings,
because of the limited number of rooms and the necessity
for an additional teacher. Where the numbers are
sufficient to form a class of a little less than ordinary
size—as a rule this kind of class should be small,—it
might be done with advantage even under ordinary
structural and staff conditions

The Highest Class

In the highest class a phenomenon commonly arises
which is very dispiriting to the class teacher. As the
scholars reach the age limit when they are no longer
under the legal obligation to attend school, they mostly
leave This is especially the case in the poorer districts.
The class, probably large at the commencement of the
educational year, gradually dwindles until towards the
close of the year there is only a mere remnant left If
the staffing arrangements permit, it is best not to disturb

the organisation, notwithstanding this almost hour-glass phenomenon Sometimes, however, it becomes necessary to blend such a remnant class with another, with the result that it usually entails further loss of scholars, besides a compulsory break in the continuity of the work The highest class, indeed, is often a most trying one on account of this leakage One good pupil follows another into the world—the poor ones mostly remain to justify the Scriptures—in a way that is most disheartening to the class teacher, who is naturally anxious that every scholar in the class should have the full benefit of the school s highest course of instruction

This leakage is educational waste, which ought not to be tolerated A keener public spirit in educational matters, and particularly a greater appreciation of the value of education on the part of the scholars' parents, would do much, in the absence of legislation on the point, to mitigate this evil In Berlin,[1] where the legal upward age limit is the same as in this country, pupils who reach the age of fourteen during the educational year are not permitted to leave school until the expiry of that year Thus the gradual breaking-up process of the highest class is non-existent there.

Specialisation.

It has been shown how essential it is that the class should fit the teacher It does not follow from this condition that the teacher must fit the class. As in the industrial world division of labour is found to be efficacious and specialisation valuable, so in school life there is a growing tendency to specialisation in the way of teaching

[1] See Report of Mr. G. Andrew to the Scotch Education Department, 1904

But before proceeding to discuss the special class, as understood here, there are one or two points of general interest concerning the fitting of the teacher to the class, which will form an appropriate introduction

The organisation being settled on the basis of fitting the class to the teacher, it seems a simple matter, assuming there is no great variation in the numbers, to allow the teacher to follow his class as it rises higher and higher in the school This plan of rotation finds its partial justification in the intimate knowledge which a teacher gains of his pupils, in the deeper interest he is likely to take in them through long association, and in the fixed moral impress he could impose, assisted by length of time This principle of rotation, however, is not sound in *general* application. Applied exceptionally, that is, in cases where the teacher is strong in moral fibre, in tact, and in disciplinary power, it has many advantages. Generally it is open to the following objections

(1) The pupils' outlook is liable to become narrowed, they being only brought into teaching contact with one mind. (2) Although not equally capable of managing with thorough efficiency every class in a school, some teachers can manage the lower classes well, and the upper ones but indifferently (3) The effect of a weak or indifferent teacher following his pupils throughout their school career would probably be disastrous to most of them (4) The moral impress of a particular class teacher, though important, is certainly not the dominant one in a good school Moral effect should rather depend on the sum of the influences that converge upon a school in its entirety

In some parts of the ordinary school work it is evident that special aptitudes on the one side and special ability on the other are desirable, since they make for the highest

efficiency. The powers and temperaments associated with
a teacher of an infant school, for example, are not
necessarily those required for the due instruction and
governance of boys and girls in the senior departments,
many of whom are in the pubescent period

The division of most elementary schools into boys', girls',
and infants' departments has roughly differentiated the
teachers on the same lines   But teachers in the same
department will, of course, be found to display differences
in moral and intellectual power, differences in power of
insight into character, differences in taste, temperament,
and degree of knowledge, which the organiser must carefully consider before assigning to each a place. His chief
aim would naturally be to put each teaching unit in that
position in which it will be able to perform the most
effective work   But there are other matters connected
with this, to which wisdom should direct his attention.
Some variety of work is almost as essential to the teacher
as the scholar   The interest of the teacher should not be
lessened by keeping him year after year to the same
standard or class, except it be to the highest class, for
which often one teacher is specially fitted. A teacher's
career might be seriously affected, and his usefulness not
adequately applied, by a cabinned experience   Some men
and women, indeed, though ostensibly unsuitable for a
particular class, will rise to the occasion in a most extraordinary way, if put to the test   Experiment therefore
with the staff is allowable, within proper limitations,
especially when variety of work is deemed necessary or
desirable.

Of course, cases will arise in which it becomes almost
imperative to allocate particular classes or particular
subjects to certain teachers specially qualified to deal with
them. A point is reached in some subjects when it

becomes necessary that the teacher should have a special knowledge, and sometimes a special aptitude joined thereto, beyond the general courses of instruction included in the Government Certificate Syllabus.

This is especially the case in practical science, art, manual training in wood and metal, domestic subjects (cookery, laundry, housewifery), and modern languages. The means employed in giving instruction in all these subjects, except the last, demand that not more than about twenty pupils[1] be allowed in one class. Practical science is taught in many educational areas by specialists, and in well equipped rooms designed for the purpose, in which every pupil has sufficient space and apparatus for independent experiment. Advanced drawing instruction is given under similar conditions in art rooms which are sometimes used as centres by scholars of neighbouring schools; whilst instruction in wood and metal work and in the domestic arts is carried on wholly at specially equipped centres, each batch of scholars attending, as a rule, one session a week for each subject.

In all these subjects the skill of the specialist, the well and suitably equipped room, and the need of individual instruction are generally recognised. It would be impracticable, even if the regular class teacher possessed the special knowledge, for him to direct and supervise this practical work ; for the numbers which form such classes

[1] In the L C C. schools the number of scholars is limited to 18 in cookery, 14 in laundry, 14 in housewifery, 20 in woodwork, 16 in metal work. For instruction in art, the general tendency has been to limit the number to 25. Most of the art rooms accommodate from 25 to 30. Similarly the practical science rooms generally accommodate about 25 pupils. The Board of Education, in a letter dated Dec 11, 1901, stated that a class for practical science should not exceed 25, unless a second teacher is employed. This letter applied to a higher elementary school.

are probably small compared with the ordinary class of
which he is in daily charge It must be noticed in
connection with this that the dual demands for small
classes and specialised teaching apply only to the older
scholars in the school, usually those from 12 years of age
upwards

The importance of practical work in education cannot be
overestimated. It has been well said by a distinguished
American that "the hand is the projected brain," for
knowledge acquired by its means becomes a *living*
thing

In lieu of girls' attending the domestic training centres
one session a week for each subject that they are studying
there, and thus causing uncomfortable breaks in their
ordinary school work, it would probably be better if each
girl devoted the last six months of her school life exclusively to training in the domestic arts. There are,
however, many difficulties in the way of the adoption of
this plan The general practice is for girls to begin their
domestic training at eleven years of age Opportunities
are thus afforded for applying and strengthening at home
the knowledge acquired at each step

There is of course no need of specialisation in the
infant department The "mothering" principle ought
to find, and most often does find, its happiest expression there, for the care and training which the
young child needs are just those which a devoted,
cultured, and intelligent mother would give Interest
should run like a gold thread through the network of the
social, physical, and mental training, based on the natural
order of a child's body and mind, and reasonably within
the range of a child's activities.

Departmental Teaching.

With regard to the senior departments, specialisation in other subjects than those already named appears to be in an experimental stage. The general practice is to have one teacher responsible for the whole of the subjects taught in one class, with variations here and there, as in the case of vocal music. In this country, and to a much larger extent in America, the practice is occasionally adopted of making each member of the staff, not responsible for a class as a whole, but responsible only for those subjects in every class which he is best fitted by knowledge and aptitude to teach. Whether this principle should be applied wholly to the senior departments in primary schools, or only to the upper classes in them, or whether it should find any justification at all, is a problem which can best be determined by experience. Local conditions and circumstances have always to be considered. Generally the *complete* application of the principle has not been a success in this country. Applied, however, only to the upper classes, it might find its true position in the elementary school.

The advantages and disadvantages of this modified specialisation—*departmental teaching*, as it is called—may be briefly summarised thus:—The gains are, (1) A teacher's work is limited to instruction in subjects with which he is best acquainted and which presumably appeal most to his tastes. (2) Interest and special knowledge in the teacher ensure good method, zealous work, and breadth of treatment (3) Scholars become more interested when facts are presented in bright colours rather than in sober greys. (4) The pupil has a better opportunity of finding his true bent. (5) Scholars are likely to get a more extended horizon by being brought daily into contact with several teachers.

On the other hand, the losses or disadvantages are, (1) Diminution of moral control by the teachers because of the extended field of work (2) Divided responsibility for a class as a whole. Even supposing one teacher is considered primarily responsible for registration, attendance, punctuality, stock, tone and discipline on account of the larger share of time given to a particular class, still his influence cannot be so great as if in sole charge. (3) Strain on the teachers Little variety in the work A more liberal staff is generally necessary, therefore (4) Scholars are more likely to take a special interest in one or more subjects to the neglect of the others. General knowledge and general training of the faculties are desirable (5) Teachers are not all qualified by tact to take every class in the school

Ungraded Room

It has been decided in many parts of the United States to have an ungraded room in connection with each school for children who are unable to maintain their standing in the regular class-room [1] This is a desirable innovation. An ungraded class ought to be in charge of a teacher of exceptional powers, since the children constituting it are, as a rule, those who by irregular attendance, mental sloth, unruliness of conduct, or other causes, have fallen considerably behind the ordinary scholars, or who need special supervision in the way of discipline It has been already said that such a class should be small because individual attention is imperative In many cases a few months' training, under conditions like these, would enable a pupil to take his place in the regular class-room It is im-

[1] Report of the Educational Commission of the City of Chicago, 1900.

portant that assignment to an ungraded room should not
be regarded either as a punishment to the scholar or a
reproach to the parent   Economical considerations arise
in connection with this device, since it generally involves
the engagement of an additional teacher

The Class-Room.

It would be refreshing both to teachers and pupils if
class-rooms could be made more interchangeable than they
generally are. Difficulties, however, present themselves
The class might fit the room so far that its accommodation
may not be exceeded   Classes and class-rooms often vary
considerably in size   When, therefore, at the commencement of the educational year, the class had been adjusted
to the room, it is not always practicable to effect even a
temporary change without a breach of official regulations
When, however, rooms and classes lend themselves to
interchangeability, it   would   be   well   to   make   use
of it

Another obstacle arises in connection with desks   It is
evident that desks suitable for the older scholars are not
equally suitable for the younger ones   The two lower
classes might change rooms occasionally so far as *desks*
are concerned—the intermediate classes might do the
same, so might the upper standards   A third limitation
to interchangeability comes in the way of general equipment, each room in this respect being supplied once
a year, in accordance with the grade of the class assigned
to it   On the whole, therefore, unless there is a spare
room designed to meet general needs, class-rooms, except
for special purposes, may be regarded as not interchangeable.

The School Hall

The central hall should not, except under stress of circumstances, be used as a regular class-room In the winter months, and at other periods of the year when the weather is inclement, the use of the hall for drill is desirable It may also be used for such silent lessons as needlework and model drawing. Of course there are other uses to which the hall may be legitimately put, but it is only being considered now from the standpoint of class instruction

The Class Teacher from the point of view of Organisation.

Some aspects of this question have already been incidentally discussed, but there are other points that demand attention. The grading of class teachers by the Board of Education has recently undergone revision The old Article 50 and Article 68 teachers, etc, are no longer so designated Teachers are now graded thus [1].—

1 Certificated teachers.
2 Provisionally certificated teachers.
3 Uncertificated teachers (the old Art 50 teachers, etc.).
4. Supplementary teachers (the old Art. 68 teachers).
5 Pupil teachers
6 Probationers [2]

The head teacher has not been specifically named here, though in small schools, besides supervisory duties, he has necessarily to be a class teacher

Some local education authorities recognise the position of head assistant in schools of abnormal size, and in mixed departments supervised by a master. In the former case, some of the minor duties which ordinarily devolve upon

---

[1] See Schedule I. and Art. 12 (a, b), Code 1901.
[2] See Art. 11 (a), Code 1901.

the head teacher are taken over by the head assistant, and
in the latter case, the head assistant mistress generally
becomes responsible for the supervision of the needlework
throughout the school.

Cæteris paribus, the class teachers should rank, in the
mind of the organiser, in the order of seniority of service,
but nothing should be allowed to interfere with the due
recognition and full utilisation of special ability associated
with a young member of the staff. It is advisable too that
every newly appointed class teacher should be considered as
under probation during the first year of service.[1]

The time which a teacher ought to give daily to his class
must depend on circumstances. Generally that time coin-
cides with the hours in which the school is in session; but
it is manifest that, in the case of specialisation applied to
the regular class-room, no teacher ought to be expected
to teach continuously during the day. Some intermission is necessary both on grounds of efficiency and
personal health—the time not employed in actual teaching
being utilised in the examination and correction of pupils'
exercises or in preparation for future lessons. In the case
of the regular class teacher, there is generally sufficient
variety in his work to give the desired relaxation, without
the necessity for further change and rest.

But no teacher who makes a true estimate of his profession, will regard the actual school hours as the fitting
limitations to his labours. As the successful artist is
absorbed by his art, or is a devotee to it, so the class
teacher should delight in his work. Successful issues for
both teacher and taught will then be assured.

[1] This is so under the London County Council.

Preparation of Lessons.

The teacher who desires to sustain the interest of his scholars must be interested himself. This interest on his part will keep him ever on the alert to add to his knowledge, and to give a new presentation of facts Preparation of lessons is therefore necessary. This can be best effected, as a rule, in the quietude of the home, or the privacy of the study. No lesson, however well prepared in the first instance, should be regarded as theoretically complete or technically perfect. Some variation ought to be introduced, in form, in dress, or other variety, each time it is repeated The new element will be found to be a vitalising power that antidotes the deadening influence of dry bones.

Whatever preparatory work is done, it should take permanent form in notes, These will be found useful to all concerned in the supervision of the school, and especially so as a guide and reference to the teacher himself And as it is not always possible to bring within the scope of one lesson all that was intended to be included in it, it is advisable for the teacher to have at his disposal a large note-book in which he can record the name of the lesson given, under date, and all the material points dealt with therein It is a mistake to make elaborate notes Let them be as brief as possible consistently with clearness, and mode of presentation And while brief generalisation in this respect is commendable, it ought not to be so wide as to leave two or more deductions open in the minds of the head teacher or inspector as to the extent or direction of the lesson. The notes should be, in other words, almost as complete a guide to the expert who has not heard the lesson, as to the teacher who gave it.

Correction of Class and Home Work

The correction of class work is an ever recurring difficulty which the good teacher, however, always manages to surmount It almost goes without saying that there is no lesson, no matter how individualistic in application, in which scholars should be left without controlling supervision and helpful guidance It is, therefore, most undesirable, unless a teacher can be relieved from teaching responsibilities for a short time—and this is the proper course—for him to correct such work in school hours when his attention is needed for other purposes. But cases arise in which sessional correction appears imperative Home lessons, for example, will need almost daily examination The books containing those lessons are brought in the morning and carried home at the close of the afternoon session. Something, therefore, must be done to meet this and similar cases that demand prompt attention Many teachers cut the Gordian knot by looking over these books during the two hours' dinner interval, but this does not meet the difficulty considered as a part of the school organisation.

There remain, however, a few courses for adoption, none of which can be regarded as quite satisfactory, except the first and last. These courses are (1) The preparation and reciting system as adopted in the United States (2) The partial employment of pupil teachers for this purpose. (3) The Hall Scripture lesson by the head teacher once a week, which ought for the time to relieve many of the assistant teachers This, however, is only, in part, a one-day remedy. (4) In certain exercises that assume a common form, exchange of books by the scholar for a few minutes for purposes of correction as guided by the teachers (5) The combination of two or more classes for a lesson in vocal music, history, etc. (6) The employment for the *details* of this work of monitors—not paid monitors, but monitors *honoris causâ*. (7) The engagement of such a liberal staff as would enable the head teacher to organise on the basis of allowing each assistant to stand off from actual teaching for, at least, one lesson every day.

But whatever course is adopted, the correction of exercises must be regarded as an important part of the work of a class teacher who, if aided in the merely mechanical side of the examination of the papers, should assess the value of each exercise himself. Too much care cannot be taken in this direction. Careless marking will re-act on the scholars, and produce destructive effects. Indeed everything that the teacher does, in this and all other school matters, ought to be a model of neatness and accuracy. Of the seven courses open to the teacher, there are one or two which ought only to be adopted in extreme cases, (4) for example. If the class teacher is an enthusiast, he will find the means of doing all the detail of correction himself, for such detail will give him an insight into each child's attainments and character, which he could not so surely obtain by any other means. The value of , this knowledge is too evident to be indicated.

Athletics.—Playground.

As the professional man's daily work cannot have a rigid time limit placed upon it, so it is with the class teacher, who should consider the school hours rather as a guide to, than a measure of, his labours:—for duties, external to the class-room, are necessarily associated with his office. Not among the least of these are (1) playground supervision, (2) supervision of scholars retained after school hours, (3) supervision of, or co-operation in, school athletics as represented by cricket and football clubs [1] etc. The first and second of these, and sometimes the third also, are usually regarded as rota work. In practice, however, athletics are best left to the direction of one inspiriting hand, who takes a special interest in them. The playground has been happily called the "uncovered school." Teachers should, in turn, exercise supervision over it at reasonable times. During the recreation interval, every teacher's place is in the playground with his scholars, directing sometimes, and occasionally taking part in, their games. A touch of *camaraderie* with pupils assists in strengthening the moral tie between teacher and taught. Besides, it helps the teacher to individualise his pupils in the way of clearer characterisation, without which knowledge real success in the management of children can never be achieved.

It is notorious that the playground brings out qualities in the pupil which may never be shown in the class-room. This alone, apart from other potent considerations, calls for the teacher's presence there.

Class Examinations.

In conformity with the practice in every good school periodical class examinations are held by the head teacher, and a record of the results preserved. It is not a rare event on occasions like these, to find that a class teacher resents any adverse criticism which the head teacher feels it necessary to make, especially when such criticism is, as it should be, recorded in a book kept for that purpose. It is well to bear in mind that the head teacher is only assessing the value of work for which he himself is responsible throughout the whole school, and that there-

[1] See Article by Mr. G. Sharples, Special Reports, Vol. 2. See also Report of the City Superintendent of New York, 1903.

London University Examinations.

DURING THE LAST SIX YEARS
5632
University Correspondence College Students
PASSED
AT THE UNIVERSITY OF LONDON,
QUALIFYING FOR
Fifty-Five University Scholarships, Exhibitions, Medals, and Prizes,
AND OBTAINING

456 Places in Honours,
Including 116 Places in First Class Honours.

Prospectus, Guide to Matriculation, Inter. Arts or Science, or B.A., Examination Pass Lists, Catalogue of College Publications, Specimen Copy of the " University Correspondent" (the College Magazine), and further particulars will be sent **post free on application** *to*

THE SECRETARY,
32 RED LION SQUARE, HOLBORN, LONDON, W.C.
SEPTEMBER 1904.

Principal of University Correspondence College.

WILLIAM BRIGGS, LL.D., M.A., F.C.S., F.R.A.S.
(*Honours in Mathematics and Law.*)

Vice-Principal.

B. J. HAYES, M.A.
(*Gold Medallist in Classics.*)

Prizes Offered

TO STUDENTS OF UNIVERSITY CORRESPONDENCE COLLEGE.

At the B.A. and B.Sc. Honours Examinations
a Prize of Ten Pounds in each Branch

will be awarded annually to University Correspondence College students taking First Class Honours.

If more U.C.C. students than one obtain Honours in the same Branch in any one year, the £10 assigned to that Branch will be divided equally among them.

Announcements of Results.

The Secretary of University Correspondence College undertakes to inform any private student, who is a candidate at Matriculation, or at the Intermediate or Degree Examination in Arts or Science, of the result of the Examination, provided that name and number, with addressed and stamped envelope or telegraph form, be sent to him at 32 Red Lion Square, London, W.C., not later than *four clear days* before the date announced for the publication of the Pass List.

Central London Laboratories.

PRACTICAL CLASSES in BIOLOGY, CHEMISTRY, & PHYSICS
in the Mornings, Afternoons, and Evenings.

Complete Intermediate Science and B.Sc. Practical Courses in the Vacations.

32 RED LION SQUARE, HOLBORN, LONDON, W.C.

The Regular Staff of Resident Tutors

By whom the Correspondence Courses are drawn up and the students' answers
corrected includes the following Graduates who obtained

FIRST CLASS HONOURS AT UNIVERSITY EXAMS. :—

C W. C BARLOW, M A. Lond. and Camb., B.Sc Lond., Gold
Medallist at M.A. Lond., Sixth Wrangler.

HARRY BATEMAN, B.A. Camb., Senior Wrangler, First Class (First
Division) in Part II. of the Math Tripos, Smith's Prizeman.

H W BAUSOR, M.A Camb, First Class in Natural Sciences Tripos,
First Class Honourman in Chemistry at Inter. Sc. Lond

WM. BROWN, M.A. Camb., Twenty-First Wrangler.

A. G CRACKNELL, M.A. Camb., B Sc Lond., F C.P., Sixth Wrangler,
First in Honours at London Matriculation.

C. S. CROSBY, M.A. Camb., Fourteenth Wrangler.

J. T. CUNNINGHAM, M A., late Fellow of University College, Oxford.

G. H. DELF, B.Sc Lond., First Class Honours in Chemistry at Inter.
Science and B.Sc.

S E GOGGIN, B A Lond., Honourman in English at Inter. Arts
and B A.

B J HAYES, Vice-Principal, M A Lond. and Camb., Gold Medallist
at M A. Lond, First Class Classic, Cambridge.

I H. HIRSCH, M A. Camb, Fourteenth Wrangler.

T. T. JEFFERY, M.A., late Fellow of St. Peter's College, Cambridge.

ALLEN MAWER, B.A. Lond. and Camb., Univ. Exhibitioner in English.

G F PERROTT, M.A. Camb., Twenty-Seventh Wrangler.

F G. PLAISTOWE, M.A. Lond and Camb., Gold Medallist in Classics,
late Fellow of Queens' College, Cambridge.

F ROSENBERG, M.A. Camb , B Sc. Lond., Sixteenth Wrangler.

JOHN SATTERLY, B Sc. Lond, First in First Class Honours and
University Scholar in Physics at B Sc

J W SHEPHERD, B.Sc. Lond., First in First Class Honours in
Chemistry at Int. Sc and B Sc , Honourman in Geology at B Sc.

W J. V STEAD, M.A. Lond, Alone in First Class Honours in
Latin at Inter. Arts, First Class Honourman in Classics at B A

W. P. STFEN, M.A. Lond., Camb., and R.U.I., Medallist in Classics

J. F. STOUT, B.A. Camb., First Class Classic.

A F. WATT, M A. Oxon., First Class Honourman at Moderations
and at the Final Classical Examination.

S. R. WEBSTER, M.A. Lond , First in First Class B.A. Honours in
French, Alone in First Class Inter and B.A. Honours in German

A J WYATT, M.A Lond and Camb , First of his year in Br IV

SPECIAL ADVANTAGES

University Correspondence College.

Tutors who have obtained the Highest Honours themselves, and who engage in no other work.

Specialists for each Subject.

Frequent dispatches of Lessons and prompt return of students' answers, forming an effective stimulus to steady work.

Full Notes to each Lesson, many of which are printed in ordinary type.

Model Answers to each Test Paper.

Fees as low as compatible with efficiency, and reduced to a minimum by the economy effected by the large number of Students working with the College. Fees (which are strictly inclusive) are payable as arranged on joining.

Transference, on payment of Registration Fee only, to a Class for the next Examination, when the Student is unavoidably prevented from going up for the Examination originally intended

Strict Privacy.

The Fees for Matric., Inter. Science, and Inter. Arts may be made to include the required Text-Books

The Fees for Preparation for the next Higher Examination are reduced to Students who pass an Examination as Members of the College.

Any Student who, after working fully through the Ordinary Course and sending up answers to each test paper within a fortnight of its receipt, fails to pass any Examination leading up to B.A. or B.Sc., will be prepared without Fee for the next Examination.

Assistance, free of charge, in obtaining scholastic posts.

Prospectus and further particulars will be sent post free on application to

THE SECRETARY,

(University Correspondence College London Office),

32 RED LION SQUARE, HOLBORN, LONDON, W.C.

fore, in all human probability, he is the last person likely
to underestimate the worth of what has been accomplished, especially as the progress books are accessible to
all inspectors The class teacher's attitude in matters of
this kind should be one of unqualified acceptance, never
doubting for a moment the justice and truth of the head
teacher's remarks Indeed this mental attitude is essential
not only to the well-being of the class but to the highest
efficiency of the teacher The head teacher's criticisms
are intended to serve the threefold purpose of estimating
progress, indicating defects, and giving helpful hints for
future guidance The teacher's art is a difficult one, and
the class teacher can only become accomplished in this
art by subordinating himself to the judgment of the head
teacher much in the same spirit as a disciple follows his
master That this is so experience points to a multitude of
examples. He who wishes to rise in his profession must not
only accept unbiassed criticism of his work as if Truth
herself had descended from her pedestal to give him a
lesson, but he must be a more severe critic of himself, of
his methods, ever undergoing self-examination, than any
head teacher or inspector could possibly be Loyal acceptance of the head teacher's views on the examination and
on all other questions that vitally concern the school, is
indispensable to easy working and successful issues

When examinations are carried out two or three times a
year by the head teacher, there does not appear to be any
necessity for similar formal examinations by the class
teacher Indeed the latter ought to be so closely in touch
with his pupils as to be able mostly to estimate their
progress by means of their daily work

It is the duty of the class teacher to preserve all records
in connection with his class. Just as a regiment, a unit in
military organisation, is proud of its deeds, so should a

class, as the unit of the school, be mindful of its achieve-
ments. To this end, a record of successes should have a
place on the class-room walls. In case of any tendency to
fall away from the ideals reached, the wise teacher will use
these records as a means of arresting depression, by calling
attention to the responsibilities of the class. Pride of
class ought to be a sentiment equally stimulating to teacher
and scholar.

Class Discipline.

Although the personality of the head teacher is responsible for the tone and discipline of a school as a whole,
which should always possess well-marked characteristics,
yet the tone and discipline of each class have their own
peculiar variations that are dependent on the *personnel* of
the class teacher. These variations should never be great;
otherwise they would be likely to disturb the balance of
the school. But the personal equation is inevitable in its
effects, and must be considered.

It may be laid down as an inviolable law, that the leading
ideas upon which are founded the tone and discipline of a
school as a whole should never be disturbed by the class
teacher. He may add to them for his pupil s good, but on
no account should he subtract from them. They should
be accepted as the foundation upon which he desires to
build. With these limitations, he has ample scope for the
display of his talents and the inductive powers of his
character.

With the improved buildings of recent years, giving
generally a separate room for each qualified assistant, the
class teacher's training influence is likely to increase. It
is, therefore, important that he should be acquainted with
the essential parts of what constitutes the perfection of
discipline—since that gives the law which governs the

school, and makes order, right conduct, and good work possible.

So far as the pupils are concerned, the tests of sound class discipline are (1) prompt and willing obedience, (2) close application, (3) pleasure in giving satisfaction to the teacher, (4) eagerness to answer questions combined with thoughtful answering, (5) good manners and right conduct generally, (6) thoroughness in work, (7) good order without unnecessary physical restraint, (8) collective and individual self-control.

On the other hand, the class teacher, in order to assist in creating these qualities and to maintain them, should be—

(1) *Patient and sympathetic* Sympathy is the key to his perfect mastery over the scholars and "patience lies at the root of all pleasures as well as of all powers."[1]

(2) *Quick in decision.* Children intuitively measure a teacher's strength, and any indecision on his part will be felt by the scholars instantaneously. The teacher, therefore, ought never to be in doubt as to the right course of action A firm but kindly exercise of power calls forth a child's respect.

(3) *True to his own commands.* It is, as a rule, a mistake to repeat an order. It is better to watch and wait until it has been fully obeyed, naming an individual or individuals if necessary. Nothing is more fatal to discipline than to allow one act of disobedience to pass—even when that act is only one of omission.

(4) *Careful to husband the voice* Loudness of speech defeats its own object, and causes a waste of energy that could be best utilised in other ways Shouting or noisy demonstration of any kind creates a bad impression The

[1] Ruskin

voice of persuasion is always natural and gentle. The teacher's eyes will aid the voice if they are used to cover the class.

(5) *Careful to sustain the children's interest*. Every step ought to be one of progress and the scholars should be made to feel it.

(6) *Just* Praise of good work or worthy conduct is valuable. Blame, on the other hand, should be used sparingly. The children must, however, feel that the teacher, above all, is just, or they will have but little respect either for his praise or his condemnation. A pupil once said of Dr. Temple (late Archbishop of Canterbury), in his successful teaching days, that he (Dr. Temple) was "a beast, but a just beast."

(7) *Consistent in his demands*. Always busy himself and always aiming at a high standard

"High endeavours are an inward light."[1]

Abundant energy at one time and slackness at another, with corresponding demands upon the scholars, are mischievous in their tendencies

(8) *Mindful that discipline is not an end, but a means to "complete living."*

(9) *Firm, self-reliant, and possessed of self-control* It is important that the scholars should understand that within the class-room lies the power of complete government. The head teacher's authority only ought to be invoked in disciplinary measures, on exceptionally trying occasions

(10) *Careful to avoid corporal punishment*, if possible. "The instruments of reformation are employment and reward—not punishment."[2]

(11) *Attentive to the scholars' physical comfort* The desk should fit the child. This point is dealt with in another place

[1] Wordsworth.   [2] Ruskin.

(12) *Always willing to give free scope for individual development* Self-expression should be encouraged It will help the teacher to form character The law of true liberty must be respected That kind of order and discipline need only to be secured which is essential to good work

"The development of soul, little else is worth study."[1]

It avails little to tell children to be good. they must be *led* in that direction One of the surest ways into the heart of a child is for the teacher to associate himself with what calls forth some of the happiest moments of its life The value of athletics in this way has already been touched upon Class rambles in town, field, and forest have equally been proved by many teachers to be a most valuable aid to good discipline

Class Registration.

This demands great care, especially because it is one of the conditions upon which grants are paid by the Board of Education Registration should be carried out in strict conformity with the Regulations As a rule, the value of a class teacher can be roughly estimated by an examination of the class register If it is kept neatly, accurately, and fully entered up to date, a favourable impression is made : if it shows that the scholars are more than usually punctual and regular in their attendance, this is, *prima facie*, due to the class teacher's influence Indeed there is no part of the teacher's duties which is more important than that of forming habits of punctuality and regularity, since these are not only an immediately valuable asset to the pupil and the school, but are likely to continue with him as a law of his life to the end of his existence Registration generally, is dealt with in the chapter on "school records."

[1] Browning

Class Excursions

Visits of the class to "places of educational value and interest "[1] as allowed by the Code, during school hours, ought to be encouraged Enterprise in this direction is generally appreciated by head teachers, who must, in the first instance, sanction such visits, and then obtain permission from H M Inspector When visits of this kind are projected, it is advisable to put the scholars beforehand in possession of the important facts concerning the objective, in order that the greatest educational value may be derived from the outing.   An effective way of doing this is to give one or more lessons on the place to be visited, and to summarise material points in a multigraphed leaflet, a copy of which is supplied to each scholar.

Conferences.

In conferences of the school staff the class teacher should take an eager interest It is advisable to hold these conferences at least once a year, preferably twice a year Presided over by a sympathetic head, always open to new ideas and fresh convictions, they generally prove a great gain to the school and a source of enlightenment to each member of the staff On these occasions, in which each teacher ought to contribute something for discussion, difficulties are threshed out and ways cleared for more rapid and certain progress.   Such conferences have been found to encourage experiment and initiative , and they therefore materially assist in maintaining that continued interest in the teachers which has been already insisted upon as essential to the interest of the scholar and the general welfare of the school

[1] Art 41 (n), Code 1904.

Pedagogy in this country has too long been regarded as a known art rather than one possessing grave difficulties and almost unfathomable depths. The theory of education involves, as Mazzini has said, the problem of human nature No man could desire a wider field for the exercise of thought and the practice of research. No class teacher, therefore, need feel that his profession is a dull one

In France, conferences pass beyond the school and take Cantonal or Departmental form All teachers in the district or area are obliged to attend the conferences, held, as a rule, twice a year, and to send in advance a contribution for discussion, either in the form of a thesis, or general impressions in the shape of notes.[1]

Sex of the Class Teacher

There remains but one other point to consider in this chapter, namely, the sex of the class teacher The German view is on the side of the employment of men even in positions which, in this country, are considered to be best filled by women. The American practice, on the other hand, goes to the other extreme, and gives largely into the hands of women teachers the education of the boys

In England, a middle course between these two has generally been followed, and thus the employment of women has been mainly limited to mixed, girls', and infants' departments

It has, however, been long felt that the change from the methods and environment of the infant department to the more rigid discipline and severer atmosphere of the senior

---

[1] See *Inspection de l'enseignement primaire*, 1900, which bears testimony to the value of these conferences The L C C. holds an annual conference of teachers to discuss pedagogical questions

schools is too great for young children, and that it
makes in the direction of retardation Experience points
to the advantage of having women teachers for Standard
I in the boys' department, and probably for Standard II
also Instances in which women teachers have had exclusive charge of boys' classes above Standard II generally
tend to prove that the combination is not quite satisfactory In mixed departments, however, where the girls
exercise a chastening influence over the boys, women class
teachers have shown themselves to be very successful even
in the upper classes There is little doubt, however, that
the elder boys are the better for being taught and guided
by a master.

CHAPTER II.

THE SCHOOL AND THE SCHOOL DEPARTMENT.

School Departments

MOST elementary schools, *provided* and *non-provided*, are organised in three departments, for boys, girls, and infants, the basis of separation being sex and age. At least both sex and age determine the separation of boys and girls from the infants, while sex only operates in forming the boys and girls into distinct departments The infants' department is invariably *mixed*, and the line of separation between it and the senior departments is one mostly of age, though attainments occasionally prevent promotion to the senior departments at the age generally required for this purpose [1] Roughly speaking, the senior departments are limited to scholars between seven and fifteen years of age,[2] and the infants' department to children between the ages of three and seven.[3]

[1] The Board of Education says, "Though no rigid rule as to age can be applied, especially in the case of delicate or afflicted children, it may be safely laid down that backward scholars of advanced age would make more progress in knowledge and form better habits in a school for older scholars than in the infant school "

[2] A scholar on attaining the age of fifteen years should have his name removed from the class register, as no grant is claimable for him after that time. He may, however, continue to receive instruction in the school until the close of the educational year in which he reached the age of fifteen See also Art 40 (n), Code 1904.

[3] The law of compulsory attendance operates at five years of age. The Board of Education has decided that children between the ages of

Although the organisation indicated above is the usual one in urban districts, several other ways of organising a school find expression in most wide educational areas, some arising from a desire of experiment and some on economical grounds Thus it is that about seven different organisations are to be found These are—

(1) Boys', girls', and infants' departments three departments

(2) Senior boys', senior girls', junior mixed, and infants' departments four departments

(3) Senior mixed, junior mixed, and infants' departments—three departments

(4) Mixed and infants' departments two departments

(5) Boys', girls and infants forming a combined department—two departments

(6) Senior mixed, junior mixed and infants forming a combined department—two departments

(7) Boys, girls, and infants, forming one department

It is usual for each department to have its own head teacher In Scotland one pedagogic head usually supervises all departments of a school In the United States the practice is to have superintendents, each of whom organises and supervises a small group of schools

The junior mixed departments, as a rule, do not have standards above III and IV.

In a school department children are grouped together according to attainments in classes varying from twenty to about eighty, the age of a child being sometimes a factor for consideration in this classification Though it

three and five should be admitted on application Refusal to admit such children can only be justified on "reasonable grounds"—See Art. 53, Code 1901 See Arts. 8, 40 (1-2), 43 (a), Code 1901.

is generally found that the majority of the children in a standard or class are approximately of the same age, yet age ought not to form the basis for classification, except in infant schools, and even there it is sometimes desirable to make exceptions

Necessity for Differentiating between Infancy and Childhood.

The necessity for differentiation in the educational treatment of infancy and childhood is based on an everyday knowledge of children and on scientific facts as revealed by physiology and psychology The infant of three years differs so much from the infant of five, and the infant of five from the child of seven, that *specially* graduated instruction is desirable Again, the four years intervening between three and seven represent a much greater difference in the rate of physical, and especially cerebral, growth than the four succeeding years The brain, according to Bain, grows with rapidity until the child is seven years old, it grows much more slowly between seven and fourteen, and more slowly still between fourteen and twenty It is desirable when cerebral growth and development are taking place at such a rapid rate in infancy, and probably putting, therefore, the child's whole system to a severe test, that the greatest care should be exercised by those responsible for the child's training During all periods of rapid growth the bodily organs become weakened, and the brain is as much a part of the physical organism as the hand Most of the vital energies are then needed for the labour of supplying increased material to the body If, therefore, the brain be stimulated into activities during the period of diminished strength arising from rapid growth, and these activities be beyond the child's powers, effects inimical to health are produced. Dr. T. B. Hyslop says diseases "are often to be traced back to an intemperate exercise of the brain functions in both psychical and motor regions during the earlier periods of development, when the greatest care and moderation are necessary."[1]

Professor Preyer also says, "The earlier the imperfectly developed central nervous system is subjected to a strain in a one-sided manner, or even in a manifold activity, so much the earlier does it become dulled, and so much the less plasticity it retains for later use."[2] Again, Professor Kirkpatrick states, "It is altogether probable that in giving children the training they will need in later life, at a time when they are in an earlier stage of development, we are, to a considerable extent, interfering with their natural order of development." Again he says, "The large number of finely adjusted movements required in making small letters accurately at an early age must result in a specialisation of the smaller nerve and muscle centres long before their natural time of development   Poor writing and drawing, which nearly always appears in about the sixth grade, may be one of the effects of lack of harmony in development, produced by the premature or excessive training of the finer muscle centres.[3]

Experience shows that mental exercises can be easily mastered by children over seven years of age which would be altogether out of place at an earlier age   This has a special application to such abstract subjects as grammar and arithmetic.

Doubtless a very close parallelism exists between physical and mental development   If growth is not to be

[1] See *The Clinical Journal*, Dec. 7, 1904.
[2] See *Mental Development in the Child*, by W. Preyer.
[3] See *Fundamentals of Child Study*, by E. A. Kirkpatrick.

retarded and development impaired, the young child must
have a varying diet suited to its bodily needs as it passes
through the various stages of growth Absence of proper
nutrition, premature, improper or over feeding, are certain
to lead to serious consequences later So it evidently is
with the brain Over-stimulation, or failure to apply the
right stimuli when needed, produces corresponding mental
effects Inner tendencies ought to be responded to at the
right times if natural development is to result The
difficulty lies in knowing exactly what kind of stimuli to
apply and when to apply them, so far as the intellectual side
is concerned The science of Pedagogy is not yet sufficiently advanced to be able to state this in exact terms , but
such knowledge as has been acquired in this direction will
be found most useful, especially when added to the close
observations of the teacher in the class-room It is known,
for example, that plasticity reaches its highest point in
early life This, then, is the fittest time to correct impressions, to form good habits and to lay the foundations
of character. It is also known that the basis of mental
power is sensory activity and that *will* development
depends mainly on motor ideas or ideas of movement
These, then, are three fundamental principles for guidance
in the instruction of infants

A young child on entering school for the first time is
generally rich in simple ideas. The whole world is before
him with its multitudes of natural sources of information
Comenius asks, "Are we not placed in Nature's garden ?
Why not turn over the living book of the world instead of
old papers ? " Before, therefore, attempting to put the child
in possession of second-hand information or knowledge
acquired by some other person, and thus, as Froebel says,
"damming up the spring of life," he should be first led
to understand and appreciate what he himself has

experienced, for in this understanding and appreciation lies the essence of all true education

The definite and adequate simple idea is the first real step in mental development "There can be no system, no order, no relationship without clearness in single things."[1] The next step is to enable the child to have easy opportunities for fresh perceptions Accurate observation, noting differences and common qualities in various objects, are essential to firm impressions Combination of simple ideas and separation of combined ideas from one another involve an advance in thought of which every ordinary child is capable, but which can, of course, be greatly strengthened by careful training

This is a mental field wide enough without introducing unnecessary abstractions Some abstraction is, of necessity, involved in these processes Trained in this way on the basis of self-discovery, a child is certain to make greater progress when the ordinary subjects of instruction have to be faced later, and to be more capable of independent mental exertion, than when the elements of the three R's are prematurely forced upon him

The question arises as to ways and means Pestalozzi, Froebel and Herbart briefly give the answer, with Froebel's voice resounding above the rest The "gifts" and "occupations" should be the principal means—in other words, play and games on an organised educational basis These tend to satisfy curiosity, the greatest force in intellectual development, and they respond to the natural desire for social intercourse Play is the preparatory school for what has to be done later in the form of work It teaches reverence for law, exercises the imagination, gives opportunities for frequent change in which every child delights, and creates little difficulties

[1] Herbart

to be mastered Indeed, play and games, without difficulties, would not be appreciated It is claimed for play and games rightly directed, that they are a means of training the senses, directing the instincts, cultivating the tastes, exciting thought, and using the emotions to form will and character

" School games involve a wide range of brain activity. Most of the senses are called into action Comparison and judgment are needed " [1]

The Pubescent Period.

From investigations made by the Child Study Department of Chicago, it appears that the pubescent age represents the period of greatest extremes in height, weight, grip and vital capacity. The pubescent age is a critical one physically and mentally, because it represents a period of rapid growth If at this period the vital energies are mainly directed to the brain, that region will not only suffer from over-stimulation, but the other organs of the body may become unequally developed Relaxation of ordinary work does not appear to be necessary : but over-strain of any kind at this period is likely to be attended with more serious consequences than at other times

Size of Departments.

What should be the size of a school department in relation to supervisory power is a question essentially administrative It has recently been laid down by the Board of Education that new schools should not, as a rule, exceed 1,200 in accommodation, that is, roughly, 400 for each department In Berlin, the accommodation of a department often ranges from 700 to 1,000 In the United States, again, particularly in New York, there are

[1] Sir William Gowers. See *The Clinical Journal*, Dec 7, 1904

schools with over 2,000 scholars supervised by one head
Looking at this question from the purely educational standpoint, in which moral development takes up a dominant
position, it cannot be denied that a sound knowledge
of the chief characteristics of each pupil on the part of the
head teacher would be of the utmost value. This knowledge can, of course, be best obtained when the area of
supervision is comparatively small   Scholars in primary
schools do not always possess those home advantages
in moral education which pupils in secondary schools
generally have.   Frequent opportunities for personal contact of the head with individual scholars are desirable,
too, on general grounds

On the other hand, the larger the school the greater, as a
rule, is the facility for perfect organisation, especially sound
classification ; it further gives each scholar a wider field in
human experience ; and assuming that the remuneration of
the head is proportional to the size of the school, a teacher
of superior attainments and ability is more likely to take
the leading part in its supervision

The Infant School.

As already stated, the law operates in the way of compulsory attendance when a child attains the age of five
years   It has, however, been a fairly general practice to
admit children when three years old if the parents so
desired, the Board of Education allowing such children to
be registered.[1]   The late School Board for London allowed
children under three years of age to be admitted to the
schools

[1] Art 43 (a), Code 1904.

Note. Children under three years of age are allowed to attend
school, but their attendances are not registered. (Parliamentary
Secretary, Board of Education, House of Commons, March 10, 1904)

In Germany and in the Netherlands there are no Municipal or State infant schools, infant instruction being left almost entirely to private enterprise In the United States infant schools such as exist in this country are not to be found There are, however, some Kindergarten schools to which infants are admitted between the ages of four and six These have only recently been established In France two institutions take the place of the English infant school, viz., the Ecole Maternelle and Infant Classes.

Écoles Maternelles.

The Écoles Maternelles [1] are State schools for children of both sexes between the ages of two and seven. The official programme states "The Ecole Maternelle is not a school in the ordinary sense of the word it is the transition from the family to the school, it retains the indulgence and affectionate gentleness of home, while initiating the child into the work and regularity of school" It further states that the efficiency must not be judged by the number of lessons and of subjects taught nor by the character of the instruction, "but rather by the sum of good influences which are brought to bear on the child, by the pleasure which he is made to take in the school, by the habits of order, cleanliness, politeness, attention, obedience and intellectual activity which he acquires, so to speak, in playing" Such schools do not provide accommodation for more than two hundred children, and are open for the convenience of parents compelled to leave home daily, from 7 a m to 7 p m in the summer, and from 8 a.m. to 6 p m in the winter The time, however, given to instruction per day is only three hours

[1] See article by Miss M S Beard, Special Reports, Vol. 8 Also Special Reports, Vol 7, p 66.

and three-quarters, and no lesson is allowed to exceed twenty
minutes in duration. The subjects of instruction comprise
(1) Moral education, (2) object lessons, (3) reading,
writing, drawing, (4) mother tongue exercises, (5) natural
history and geography, (6) hand and eye training exercises,
(7) singing and physical exercises, (8) recitation. This
formidable array of subjects is arranged on the time-table
on the principle that change is rest. there is, besides, an
intermission of a few minutes between each lesson, and
children under five years of age are not taught reading
and writing.

Provision is made on the premises for giving the
children their meals either on payment or gratuitously,
according to the circumstances of the parents. Women
helpers other than teachers assist in this work and give
all desirable attention to the health and cleanliness of the
scholars. Among the Parisian schools of this type each
teacher has charge of about 50 children

Infant Classes

The infant classes (*Classes Enfantines*) are of two kinds,
one serving to bridge over the gap between the *école maternelle* and the ordinary primary school, and usually found
in large towns, the other existing in rural districts, and
corresponding mainly in age limitations and subjects of
instruction to the infant schools in this country.

Kinderhorte, etc.

In Berlin and Charlottenburg,[1] associated with the
more recent school buildings, there are rooms (*horte*)
reserved for children, who need at least quasi parental

[1] See Report of Mr. G. Andrew to the Scotch Education Department, 1904

attention The children can remain in these rooms, which partake of the nature of a crêche, from 2 to 7 p.m., under the charge of superintendents Play and preparation of lessons are the chief means of employment Meals are supplied under similar conditions to those associated with the *écoles maternelles* The school authorities, as a rule, lend the rooms, while the upkeep is provided by private benevolence

The crêche has now become a reality in most European countries and in America Its existence, however, in most places, appears to depend on private effort Mr. Hilton's crêche, established in 1871 at Stepney Causeway, showed how successfully and usefully such institutions could be worked This crêche still exists, and is open from 7.30 a m to 7 30 p m Children from three weeks to five years old are admitted daily Great care is taken to see that all admitted are free from infection, etc There is every reasonable provision for health and comfort, and there are all the usual accessories for play Cots are provided for infants The staff consists of a matron and trained nurses

From the standpoint of school attendance *alone* the crêche is a useful institution, since boys and girls who ought to be at school are often kept at home for nursing duties while the mother is necessarily at work. On humanitarian grounds, however, the crêche's highest functions may be said to rest

Infant Schools in this Country.

The English infant school is invariably mixed, and classification is based principally upon age Originally these schools were intended to confine their instruction to purely infant needs, but congestion in senior departments and organisation demands have sometimes necessitated the

62   THE SCHOOL AND THE SCHOOL DEPARTMENT

retention of children in the infant department after they
have reached the age to be drafted to the senior schools
Such children are usually formed into a Standard I class,
and in some cases even into a Standard II class

The Board of Education says, " Scholars who, at the close
of the course of instruction for the year, will not have completed their seventh year, should generally be regarded as
infants." [1]

Accepting this definition of an infant as applied to
all departments in which there is no Standard I , and
assuming that children enter school between three and
four years of age, it is evident that a three years'
course of instruction ought to be arranged Clearly,
it is desirable to have separate classes for each year's
course, but in small schools this is not always practicable,
and a modified syllabus must then be adopted Supposing,
however, a department has sufficient children to make
three classes, each with its own teacher, the organisation
becomes simple, and usually assumes the following form,
if there is a fairly equable distribution of children in regard
to age.

Class	Age of children at close of educa-tional year.	General attainments[2] at close of educa-tional year.
Class 1.	Over six	Such as would enable the children to commence the work of Standard I

[1] In the L.C C Provisional Code 1904 there is the following note :
" Teachers should bear in mind that, as a rule, children who have turned
six and seven years of age, should be able to commence the work of
Standards I and II respectively at the beginning of the educational
year "
[2] This arrangement represents the usual practice; but each head
teacher must judge for herself what the nature of the attainments
should be

| Class ii | Over five | Such as would enable the children to commence the work of Class i That is, Class ii should represent two removes from Standard I |
| Class iii | Over four | Such as would enable the children to commence the work of Class ii That is, Class iii should represent three removes from Standard I |

In large infant departments there are as many as ten or twelve classes The common practice has been to number these classes from one to ten or twelve—Class 1 being the highest—which in the absence of a knowledge of the courses of instruction associated with each class is very misleading; whereas the adoption of a suggestive nomenclature like that indicated below would place everyone in possession of the approximate position of the class, without referring to the curriculum If there are six classes in an infant school, two containing children who will be over six years of age at the end of the year, two with those who will be over five, and two with those who will be over four, the best nomenclature is one representing yearly steps, thus—

Class i (A)   Class ii (A)   Class iii (A)

Class i. (B)   Class ii (B)   Class iii. (B)

Similarly, if there are nine classes,—

Class i (A), Class i (B), Class i (C), and so on

Some confusion has arisen in the past through the want of a common nomenclature like this For example, sometimes Classes i , ii., and iii have all been found in large infant schools to represent Class i , or one remove from Standard I., in one year, whereas in another year Class iii. might represent two removes The simple nomenclature set out here is constant in meaning, suggestive in form, and capable of permanent and general application.

Another plan, perhaps a better one, is to call each class a grade [1]

Grade i would then be the lowest class—three removes from Standard I

Grade ii would be the next highest class—two removes from Standard I

Grade iii would be the highest class—one remove from Standard I

For two or more classes in the same grade the lettering should be used, as already shown

As it often happens that children are admitted to infant schools over five or six years of age who have had no previous systematic training, it becomes a difficult matter to allocate them to suitable classes, especially so when such admissions take place at an advanced period of the educational year   This ever-recurring difficulty accentuates the need for an ungraded room to which such children could be sent, at least for a few months

From the point of view of general efficiency it is probably desirable instead of admitting children at all times and seasons, only to allow admissions at two stated periods of the year.   Certain exceptions would, of course, have to be made to this arrangement to meet such special cases as removal of parents from one district to another.

The Kindergarten

The ordinary infant school varies greatly as to the amount and kind of Kindergarten work that is done

[1] This is adopted in the United States, where the grades, beginning with the lowest class (Grade i) in the Kindergarten, are continued throughout the Senior schools.

within its walls Some head teachers regard this
kind of instruction as essential, and give up most if not
all of the time to it in the lower parts of the school;
others, again, are content to devote but a few hours a
week.

The Kindergartens are almost exclusively devoted to
the principles of instruction underlying Froebel's teaching
Everything, therefore, is of a practical character The
Kindergartens of Germany are mostly private institutions.
In America, where under State aid the Kindergartens are
rapidly increasing in number, the children attend school
in the mornings only as a rule, while in the afternoons the
teachers devote their time to visiting the parents in order
to enlist their sympathy and co-operation in the work
of the schools. These visits, too, enable the teacher
to get through the mother an intimate knowledge of
a child's peculiarities In the American Kindergartens
about twenty-five children form a class in charge of one
teacher. In like manner, at the Kindergarten School,
Froebel Institute, London, W, no class is allowed to
exceed 25 scholars

Age is, of course, the chief basis of classification in these
schools A transition department, between the Kindergarten and the regular primary school, is to be found in
various places.

Inter-Departmental Promotion.

Promotion has been already briefly discussed except in
its inter-departmental aspect The rules for inter-departmental promotion in operation in London County Council
schools appear to work satisfactorily. They are given below in their main characteristics, and will probably be
found useful as a guide in meeting local peculiarities

" Promotion from Infants' departments to Senior departments should be made at the beginning of the educational year, and should consist of : —

In schools where there is no Standard I in the Infants' department —

(i) All children who in the opinion of the head teachers and managers are fit to commence the work of Standard I , and

(ii) All children who will become seven years of age during the first half of the educational year

In schools where there is a Standard I in both the Infants' and the Senior departments —

(i) All children who in the opinion of the head teachers and managers are fit to commence the work of Standard II , and

(ii) All children who will become eight years of age during the first half of the educational year

In schools where there is no Standard I in the Senior department —

(i) All children who in the opinion of the head teachers and managers are fit to commence the work of Standard II

(ii) All children who will become nine years of age during the educational year

Promotions from Infants' to Senior departments may, in exceptional cases, also take place at the end of January This should be a promotion for ability, and should be made only on the following conditions —

(i) That there is sufficient room in the Senior departments, and that the admission of children from outside will not be seriously impeded (ii) That no undue strain will be thrown on the staff and classification of the Senior school.

(iii) That the staff of the Infant school be adequately employed with the remaining children

In schools where there is a Standard I in both the Infants' and the Senior departments, all applicants for admission who will be under eight years of age at the end of the educational year current at the time of admission must be admitted into the Infants' department, and those who will be over eight years of age at the end of that educational year must be admitted into the Boys' or Girls' department.

When transferring Infants to Senior departments, the head teachers of Infants' departments must send the following form, properly filled up, to the head teachers of the Senior departments one week prior to the date of transfer.—

Name. (Surname first)	Date of Birth as recorded			Class in Infants' Department	Date of Admission to Infants' Department	Address.
	Day	Month	Year			

There must be an examination of the children whom it is proposed to promote at the end of the educational year. This examination must take place in the Infants' department before the summer holidays, and must be conducted jointly by the Infants' head teacher and the head teacher of the Junior Mixed or Senior department concerned.   It

is desirable that the class teacher who has actually taught
the children should be present at the examination, to whose
opinion some weight should be attached The object of the
examination should be to ascertain which of the children
may beneficially proceed to the first or second standard
without danger of overpressure A classified list of the
children, signed by the head teacher of the Infants' department, should accompany them when transferred to the
Junior Mixed or the Senior departments, and be preserved by
the head teachers of the latter, who are, however, authorised
to classify individual children otherwise than in the list on
entering the cases with their reasons in the log book.

Promotions from Junior Mixed to Senior departments
are to be made at the commencement of the educational
year, and are to consist of—

(i) All children who, in the opinion of the head teachers
and managers, are fit to commence the work of the lowest
Standard in the Senior department.

(ii.) All children who will become ten during the first
half of the educational year, or if there is no Standard III.
or IV. in the Senior department, then those who will
become eleven or twelve years respectively

(iii) The same procedure as to examination, etc., is to
take place in the case of promotions from Junior Mixed
departments as in the case of promotions from the Infants'
department."

Co-education v. Separation

Separation of the sexes versus co-education. Much discussion has taken place concerning the relative merits of
these two systems In America co-education has been in
operation a long time, and, it is claimed, with highly beneficial results In Scotland mixed schools are common,
owing probably to the influence of Stow. Co-education,

too, is the general rule in Holland and Switzerland. Many
other countries also accept the principle of co-education
when applied to rural districts where the population is
small, but economy in these cases is probably the determining factor.

In this country co-education has been extended considerably in recent years, but the separation of the sexes,
as in Germany and Hungary, is fairly general in the
towns Junior mixed schools appear to be outside the
area of controversy, as their utility is mostly recognised
Their curricula are similar to the *Cours élémentaire*[1] in
France, but sometimes wholly or partially cover the *Cours
moyen*. Also junior mixed departments[2] in which women
are mostly engaged as class teachers are valuable as a
transition between the infant department and the senior
boys' or girls' school.

Pros. and Cons.

The advantages of the separation of the sexes in education are—

(1) Neither boys nor girls are retarded in subjects for
which they respectively show natural aptitudes (2) There
are fewer breaks in the work of a class as a whole than
when boys and girls are mixed Cookery, laundry,
housewifery, needlework take the girls away from the
ordinary school work several times a week—especially the
elder girls

[1] In France the elementary schools have three grades, standards
or steps, viz. *Cours élémentaire, Cours moyen, Cours supérieur*. These
correspond respectively with the ages 6 to 9, 9 to 11, 11 to 13.

[2] " Part of the instruction of infants should be given by means of
appropriate and varied occupations, *and to a less extent, the same methods
should find a place in the teaching of the younger scholars.*" —Note to Art.
1, Code 1904

(3) The discipline that is suitable for a boy is not, as a rule, equally suitable for a girl   (4) The boy is more likely to get a virile character under the sole direction of a master; and the girl would be more likely when trained by mistresses to develop that sweetness of disposition which generally distinguishes the best of her sex.

(5) The curriculum can be better arranged, without give and take, to suit the needs of boys and girls and the different ends in view in their education   (6) The field of a woman's work is, as a rule, very different from that of a man's Cultivation of the qualities essential to each is better secured by separation

The advantages of co-education appear to be—

(1) Co-education is an aid to organisation in small schools; it is also an aid to classification in general subjects in all schools.

(2) It produces a spirit of camaraderie between the sexes

(3) It exercises a chastening influence on the boys and makes them less self-conscious   The girls too become more self-reliant.

(4) The boys show a greater respect for girls and women

(5) Discipline is more easily obtained.

(6) Boys are put more upon their mettle, as they have to compete with the girls natural qualities of patient endeavour and steadiness of aim

Co-education may be considered to be in an experimental stage in this country.   So far, mixed schools have fully justified their existence.   Mixed evening schools are generally more successful than those that are not mixed

If co-education is consistent with Nature s methods, as

it seems to be, it is bound sooner or later to take up a
strong position and assert its dignity and influence
everywhere National characteristics, however, must always
be a factor for consideration in dealing with this interesting
problem.

Principles of Staffing.

Every school must have a " sufficient and suitable staff "
In determining the sufficiency and suitability of the staff
consideration must be given to, (1) The nature of the
premises generally—number and size of class-rooms and
their distribution (2) The number of scholars in habitual
attendance (3) The age and attainments of the scholars
and the mode of classification (4) The character of the
courses of instruction, with special reference to practical
work (5) The ability of the teachers and their status [1]

Minimum sufficiency is determined thus [2].—

The head teacher [3] is considered equivalent to fifty
children in average attendance.

A certificated teacher is considered equivalent to sixty
children in average attendance

An uncertificated or provisionally certificated assistant
is considered equivalent to forty-five children in average
attendance

A supplementary assistant is considered equivalent to
thirty children in average attendance

A pupil teacher [4] is considered equivalent to thirty
children in average attendance

A probationer [4] is considered equivalent to twenty
children in average attendance

[1] See Art 11 and Schedule I , Code 1904.
[2] See Art 12 (a) and warning note, ibid   [3] See Art 9, ibid
[4] Recognition of probationers ceased after August 1, 1904, but
probationers recognised under previous Codes will continue to be

In regard to most schools, in which there is but little variation in habitual attendance, the staff for any year is usually determined, *ab initio*, on the basis of the average attendance of the previous year.

Special staffing arrangements are made by the Board of Education for schools in areas with a small population. [1]

The minimum staff scale, as set out here, has evidently been adopted with many peculiar circumstances and a variety of conditions in view. It is not intended to suit modern buildings with separate rooms for each class, but is rather an indication of the lowest ebb to which a staff may fall, and then only acceptable as a condition of efficiency.

It has been pointed out in the previous chapter how desirable it is to have a staffing basis much more generous than this scale demands. Having regard to the warning note in the Code, it is manifestly the wish of the Board of Education that schools should, as a rule, be staffed more generously than the scale indicates.

The usual scale applied by the Education Authority for London is approximately one certificated teacher for every fifty children in average attendance, the head teacher, centre instructors, visiting teachers, and pupil teachers not being reckoned for this purpose. In practice, however, for there are cases in which the class-rooms are mostly small—accommodation varying from forty to forty-eight—the staff works out as a whole at one certificated assistant for an average of about forty-six [2] children in attendance.

recognised until the date at which then recognition would cease in the ordinary course. See Schedule III, Regulations for the Instruction and Training of Pupil Teachers, 1903.

[1] See Art. 12 (*b*) and Art. 32, Code 1904.

[2] The West Lambeth Teachers' Association is asking that classes in infant and senior departments be limited to a roll of forty and thirty respectively.—See *The Schoolmaster*, Jan. 7, 1905.

Theie is no fixed scale in force for the Council schools. The existing practice has grown out of general policy, pointing to an unwritten law capable of some elasticity to suit the circumstances of each school.[1]

Staffing Difficulties in Schools of Old Type.

School buildings of the old type, often with a room eighteen feet wide and any length, or with one room in the form of a hall without even the suspicion of a class-room, present grave difficulties to the teaching staff. Though some of these buildings are still in existence and in use, unaltered save by the hand of time, most of them have undergone structural changes that render the work of education both easier and more efficient. In the absence of permanent structural alterations, devices for the separation of the classes have been adopted, these mostly assuming the form of curtains or dwarf portable partitions. By these means, and by a careful distribution of quiet and noisy lessons among the various classes, strains have been lessened and activities economised. The evils attendant on these antiquated premises have been somewhat accentuated by the general employment of uncertificated teachers, who, through the comparatively small number of children they were officially regarded as competent to teach, have necessarily increased the number of contending voices in a school. Many of these teachers possess excellent powers of discipline and sound instructive ability; but when a certain number of children, representing several classes, must occupy one room, it is, of course, preferable to have two teachers talking at the same

[1] "The staff of a school is fixed by the Committee, after having given due consideration to the circumstances of each school."—L.C.C. Provisional Code 1904.

time rather than three or four. Hence, on this ground only, apart from considerations of superior knowledge and skill, it is desirable to have certificated teachers employed.

Teachers Giving Partial Time or Visiting Teachers.

Exigencies of school life sometimes demand the employment of occasional teachers, that is those giving partial time. In the case of a mixed school presided over by a master and without the permanent aid of an assistant mistress a woman must be engaged to give the necessary instruction in needlework. In like manner, a drill instructor is sometimes engaged to superintend the physical side of the scholars training.

Of recent years there has been a tendency towards specialisation in certain subjects. Visiting teachers have therefore greatly increased in number. These are mostly employed in giving instruction in science, art, and modern languages, their work being supplemented by members of the ordinary staff.

Pupil Teachers

Pupil teachers may now be generally regarded as giving partial time to actual school work. Arrangements for the training of pupil teachers have varied so much in different educational areas, the variations being especially great in voluntary schools, that it is not proposed to summarise them here. The practice in large towns has generally been, however, fairly uniform the pupil teacher spending one half of the week in school and the other half at the centre or pupil teachers' school. This practice has been confirmed by the recent regulations for the instruction and training of pupil teachers which came into partial operation on

August 1st, 1904   The regulations,[1] in the words of the Prefatory Memorandum, "are intended to secure for the pupil teacher a more complete and continuous education, and to make the period of service in an elementary school a time of probation and training rather than of too early practice in teaching"

It is undesirable for pupil teachers to be held entirely responsible for a class   the staff ought to be sufficient and suitable without this aid, and the school should be adapted for their training   At the same time practice in teaching is essential   This can be secured by a systematised course of criticism lessons, and by allowing the pupil teacher to have charge of a small portion of a class for a short time under the direct supervision of the head teacher or a certificated assistant   When not so engaged, he should have as much variety of teaching as possible with other classes in the school, the upper standards being generally excepted, and be brought into close contact with school routine Without a sense of increasing responsibility and growing power in the management of children and a fair knowledge of the conditions of general and individual progress, the training of a pupil teacher in the art of teaching cannot become a reality   A properly graduated course of school training, increasing in difficulty and scope as the articled time advances, ought to be a part of the working scheme of every school having pupil teachers · "Registers[2] showing the time spent by each pupil teacher in this training, and full records of its nature, must be kept by the head teacher of the school   [3]

[1] "After August 1st, 1905, pupil teachers will not be permitted to serve in a public elementary school more than half the time the school is open "—Regulations for the Instruction and Training of Pupil Teachers, 1903   [2] Art 3, ibid

[3] "After August 1st, 1905, no boy or girl will be allowed to take any part in the management or instruction of a class until the age of 16

Absences of Teachers

The absences of teachers through illness and other transient causes are generally disturbing elements in the life of a school. The extent of the disturbance, however, depends greatly on the numerical and qualitative strength of the staff. The department that is staffed only up to minimum requirements naturally feels these disturbances most keenly, whereas generous staffing arrangements enable the head teacher to fill up the gap promptly. If the head teacher is not otherwise tied to a class it is his duty to fill up the vacant position, supposing no other qualified member of the staff is available.

It, however, often happens that the hands of each teacher are otherwise full; and as a class must be controlled and taught, it becomes necessary to devise some temporary expedient for meeting the emergency. Such expedients must, of course, vary according to circumstances. In practice they often involve a departure from the time table, which should be avoided if possible. All departures from the time table should be logged and the circumstances stated. It goes without saying that the wisest course to pursue is the one that involves the least deviation from every-day practice, and also fairly meets the needs of the teacherless class.

This is generally effected by an alternation of private study (or any quiet individual work such as writing and drawing) and class teaching in two adjoining classes, the one teacher, with such minor aids as are ordinarily available in a school, distributing oral lessons over the two classes, and also guiding private effort and testing its results as far as possible. The occasional practice of putting two classes into one room and overcrowding it must be condemned.

(or in rural districts 15).—" Prefatory Memorandum, Regulations for the Instruction and Training of Pupil Teachers, 1903."

When, however, a commodious room is available into which the two classes can be conveniently put, oral lessons might be given to the combined class in certain subjects, if the attainments of scholars are not widely different ; or, as in the other instance, private study and oral lessons might alternate

Other devices are sometimes practised, under stress of circumstances, not always in conformity with the spirit of official regulations It is pleaded in these cases that necessity knows no law, and that an unduly severe view cannot be taken of an exceptional position of a temporary character that has, all things considered, been met in a reasonable manner.

Supply Teachers.

But all the inconveniences caused by the absences of teachers point to the wisdom—when there is no organised system of "supplies" prompt in filling up vacancies, especially sudden and unexpected ones—of giving each department a marginal or liberal staff. This is apparently done to a large extent in the United States "It is universally recognised," says Mr. W C. Fletcher in the Report of the Mosely Education Commission, 1904, " that teachers should not be actually teaching all through the school day 20 or 22 periods of actual teaching out of 30 seem about the general rule " Again, Mr G Andrew, in his Report to the Scotch Education Department on the Schools of Berlin and Charlottenburg, says, " A teacher gives, as a rule, from 24 to 28 hours' instruction in a week, out of a possible 32 hours "

Voluntary schools in the past have suffered more through the absences of teachers than the Board schools, because the latter in most large areas had a system of " supply " teachers, and were, as a rule, much more liberally staffed

But now that both Council and non-provided schools are under the direction of the same local authority, which is responsible for their efficient management, there should be no valid reason why both classes of schools should not equally profit by an organised system of "supplies"

Under the London County Council there is a "supply" system [1] The "supply" teachers are divided into two classes—

(1) "Unattached" teachers who may be sent to any school in London to fill a temporary vacancy, and who are under the direct control of the head office

(2) "Supply" teachers under the orders of the local or divisional correspondent, who may send them to any school within his jurisdiction to fill occasional vacancies of a temporary character

The Head Teacher.

The Head Teacher is generally teacher, director, and superintendent His opportunities for good are great and many His responsibilities are, therefore, commensurate therewith No one could desire a more responsive field for sowing good seed than that represented, as a rule, by the scholars of a school The head teacher's influence must depend primarily on his strength of character

In order that the sum of his influences may be great over both staff and pupils, the following are the chief qualities and powers it is desirable for him to possess (1) lofty sense of duty; (2) broad sympathy—not willingly "to brush the down from a butterfly's wing"; (3) sound judgment ; (4) power of insight into character , (5) love of his work , (6) originality or initiative, and belief in "the continual law of progress "; (7) self-control , (8) organising power; (9) firmness , (10) persuasive powers of

[1] This only applies to the Council schools at present,

speech, (11) general purity of character, and (12) ability
to breathe the spirit of it into the school   Of course this
array of qualities is somewhat ideal   A detailed knowledge of school work is presumed

It should be borne in mind that every head teacher
worthy of the name is generally regarded by his scholars
as an ideal personality possessing extraordinary knowledge,
and gifted, too, beyond the run of ordinary mortals
Honour, justice, truth are presumed to govern all his
actions This general and illimitable faith in him, combined with the reality of his own powers, are forces which
he can direct to perfect the organisation and control of his
school   The greatest care and circumspection are of
course necessary if the scholars' ideal is to remain un-
sullied and unshattered amidst the daily provocations to
which he is subjected.   Self-watchfulness ought to be
his constant sentinel

The principal duties of the head teacher are included in
(1) organisation, (2) supervision, (3) teaching, and (4)
examination, or, to use official phraseology, "the general
control and supervision of the instruction and discipline."
The special aim of the school, its size, the number and
capabilities of the assistant teachers are factors in
determining a wise distribution of time over these various
parts of a head teacher's work.

The salient features of organisation are too evident to
be indicated in connection with this matter, but two or
three points are worthy of note in this place   Although
the word "standard" has been deleted from the Code so
far as it applies to classification, the standards are still
retained in name and scope as *standards of examination for
certificates of proficiency*   In practice, however, they are
still used to define courses of instruction applicable to
classes, though there is much evidence of freedom from

the trammels they originally imposed. The liberty of
unrestricted classification—*unrestricted*, that is, within
reasonable limits—has been utilised by the adoption in
suitable cases of intermediate courses between one standard
and another, and by other departures from the old lines,
making for greater changes still. But in this respect each
school must discover for itself what courses are best suited for
its own development, as local circumstances vary so greatly.

Sometimes a classification is adopted based on attainments and aptitudes of scholars in one or more subjects,
as distinguished from their general attainments in *all* subjects—this latter being the basis on which classes are
usually organised. For example, the school being arranged
in classes according to general attainments, a scholar in,
say, Standard IV. may possess exceptional talent in
drawing, and have but poor ability in *number*. The head
teacher can then, if he pleases, allow this scholar to receive
instruction in all other subjects in Standard IV and place
him for drawing in Standard VI and for arithmetic in
Standard II. Indeed the whole school may be organised
on this plan. In practice, however, it is found not to
work well, as a rule, in an elementary school, if extensively
applied. Probably the best application of this principle of
cross classification—as it may be called—is a very limited
one founded on the few cases of exceptional ability in a
certain direction on the one hand, and one-sided dulness on
the other, which are invariably present in every school.

Departmental teaching, already referred to in the last
chapter, founded on the apparently logical basis of subjects
rather than classes, is somewhat allied to this system of
cross classification, inasmuch as both are founded on
subjects. In the former case the subject is primarily
associated with the teacher, and in the latter case with
the scholar.

Supervision cannot, of course, be complete, and must indeed be defective, when the head teacher is solely responsible for a class. The degree, therefore, with which this can be carried out must depend on the amount of school freedom he possesses. An able and liberal assistant staff will confer all the liberty he can reasonably desire. It is a mistake, however, to allow even supervision to be too engrossing—to be a gulf swallowing up most of the time—for colleagues should be trusted until they are found wanting, and supervision merely involves a general, and only *occasionally a particular*, watchfulness over the application of syllabuses, methods of instruction, home lessons, discipline, and degree of observance of organised plans generally.

It ought not to be necessary for any head teacher, possessing firmness of decision and ordinary force of character, to repeat his requests or orders twice, before being accepted and applied by every member of the staff. Besides, excessive supervision is not conducive to that good relationship between head and assistants which ought to characterise every school. Young and inexperienced assistant teachers, of course, need more supervision and guidance than others.

One of the most important functions that a head teacher is called upon to discharge is that which refers to actual teaching. A certain amount of time per week, about ten or twelve hours, ought, as far as possible, regularly to be given to this work. It is inadvisable for the head teacher to confine his attentions in this respect to one or even two classes—assuming that there are many classes—but to distribute his teaching over the whole school from time to time, giving weak spots and the upper classes, particularly the first class, a little more of his individuality and power than the others. The intimate relationship between the head and the scholars established by this direct teaching puts him into more sensitive communication with the pulse of the school. He can better estimate by this means the value of the moral and intellectual training which the pupils are generally receiving than by mere examination, which, after all, only brings out the less important side of a good education These lessons, too, ought to serve as models in method, breadth of view, and fulness of knowledge for the guidance and example of the assistant staff, in addition to their value in extending and colouring the horizon of the scholars

In Germany and the United States it is a general practice for head teachers, even of very large schools, to give about one-third of their time to actual class teaching. "The Rektor (head teacher), apart from his general supervision of the school, performs usually twelve hours' teaching a week He does not always teach either the same subject or the same class, but varies his work every school semester."[1]

School Examinations.

Examination, essential for obtaining exact information as to progress, should be systematised The usual practice is to divide the year into two or three terms and give an examination towards the close of each, based, of course, on the syllabuses. Occasional tests are also advisable in certain subjects, especially if there is a weak spot in the teaching staff

[1] Report of Mr. G. Andrew to the Scotch Education Department on the Primary Schools of Berlin and Charlottenburg, 1904.

In Kansas City " the head teacher is usually responsible for a class, and thus exercises relatively little supervision over the work of a school "—Report of the Rev A W. Jephson, issued by the late School Board for London, 1904

The regular term examinations[1] assume individual form in the three R's, and *class* form, mostly, in the other subjects, except in the upper classes, in which it is found generally desirable to secure written tests in such subjects as lend themselves to those means.

The possibility of holding these examinations is hardly worthy of discussion, provided circumstances are normal. In a liberally staffed school no difficulties ought to arise; but in schools where the head teacher is responsible for a class a temporary interchange of classes between the head and the assistant whose class is to be examined has its weak points, though it is generally found to work fairly satisfactorily.

In all these examinations it is most important that the head teacher (1) *should set the tests and questions himself*. in some cases, particularly when the class teacher is a specialist in a certain subject, it is desirable either for the head teacher to consult him before finally deciding on the questions, or to allow *him* to draw up the questions, and for the head to approve their ultimate form; (2) *should be careful that they are reasonable tests*, having regard to the period of the year and the attainments of the scholars at its commencement; (3) *should personally and strictly supervise the examination*, (4) *should examine all the papers himself*: this will give him a close knowledge of the state of things he could not otherwise possess; (5) *should allow each scholar to see his paper after correction*, so that errors may be known and right ideas substituted; (6) *should record the degree of proficiency* by a mark or symbol, in a schedule or book kept for that purpose, in the case of all individual tests, and a written

<hr>

[1] These are in accordance with the Revised Instructions of 1903 to H.M. Inspectors. See (d) *Examination of School Work*, Prefatory Memorandum, Code 1904, and also Art 22.

assessment and criticism in class subjects; (7) *should see that his standard of desirable attainments is a reasonably high one,* and (8) *take immediate steps to remove or remedy any glaring class deficiencies or weaknesses* revealed by the examination.

Above all, the head teacher must bear in mind the peculiar position in which he is placed by these examinations — called upon to judge the work for which he is primarily responsible and to record the judgment in writing. It is therefore a position of great trust and one that deserves to be met by corresponding sincerity and candour. The presence therefore in the head teacher's mind of the true spirit of justice and a complete absence of self-interest ought to direct him through every stage of the examination and companion him in assessing the results and in recording his criticisms, which, needless to say, should be fearless and impersonal. In other words, he ought to weigh the results and test their educational value like a fair-minded expert estimating the work of an unknown person. Ultra sensitiveness of the staff or any part of it to adverse criticism of its work should not be considered. There is, however, a gentle and a rough way of telling the truth. The wise head teacher will know which to choose.

A generous or over estimate of the value of the work accomplished will defeat the object which prompted such folly, while any suppression or covering of ugly truths must prove the sowing of "dragon's teeth," the self-gathering harvest of which must inevitably come later. The welfare of the school and the interests of the head teacher and staff are best served in discovering the truth and telling it in a plain way.

Curriculum and Time Table. In determining each of these, due consideration should be given to (1) the Code,[1]

---

[1] See Arts. 1 to 7, Code 1904.

the letter and spirit of which will be found to be an
admirable guide. Certain subjects will be found therein
to all intents and purposes to be *obligatory*, though reasonable latitude is allowed to meet exceptional cases. The
Herbartian principle[1] of unification of subjects is recognised as "desirable" in a limited way. Froebel's insistence
upon practical work also comes in for recognition, not only
in the case of infants, but also as applied to "younger
scholars" (2) The class of children, their sex, ages,
and attainments. (3) The quality of the staff. (4)
Building and equipment. (5) Times of meeting. (6) Local
circumstances generally. In agricultural districts, for
example, it is desirable that the elementary principles of
agriculture and horticulture should be taught. There is,
too, in this instance a wide field for Nature study. In the
French and German country schools these subjects receive
generally a conspicuous share of attention.[2]

But apart from local circumstances there are certain
subjects whose influence upon the scholars' lives after the
school career has ended cannot but be considered as great
and beneficial. These are English literature and Civics,
both of which occupy an important place in the curricula
of schools in America.[3] A further point to consider is the
desirability of making the instruction in all subjects, as
far as possible, essentially practical. If this is done, a
more limited curriculum would be necessary than is usually
found in primary schools, since practical work involves
more time than the merely theoretical. "The School of
Education" at Chicago presided over by Dr. Dewey is an ex-

[1] That subjects of instruction should be so connected and associated
with one another that the child's ideas should be bound together in
circles of thought.
[2] See Special Reports (Mr. Sadler's), Vols. 7 and 9.
[3] See Reports of the Mosely Education Commission.

pertinent, and is being run entirely on practical lines.[1] There can be no doubt of the importance of insisting that what a child learns theoretically to-day he should be taught as far as possible to apply to-morrow, or, better still, the child should have the means of discovering the application for himself. All the great educational theorists from Bacon to Herbert Spencer may be said substantially to have promulgated this view[2] The Real Schools of Germany may be said also to be partially founded upon it

In the Code of 1903, Article 15 (a) states "The course of instruction in infant schools and classes should, as a rule, include—

Suitable instruction in reading, writing, and numbers
Simple lessons on common things
Appropriate and varied occupations
Needlework
Drawing
Singing
Physical Training"

This syllabus is omitted in the Code of 1904[3] There is, however, an evident intention that no great departures should be made from it, at present

Time Tables.

Caeteris paribus, the easy working of a school will depend a great deal on the suitability of the Time Table, which

[1] See Report of the Mosely Education Commission, pp. 203 and 356 : articles by Mr. J. R Heape and Mr. A J Shepheard

[2] "The school must encourage to the utmost the children's natural activities of hand and eye by suitable forms of practical work and manual instruction "—Introduction to Code 1904

[3] The Prefatory Memorandum of this Code says: "It is not desirable that any far-reaching changes in the instruction now given in the schools should suddenly be made " This probably foreshadows a great change in infant methods and practice Froebel's principles will probably dominate all infant schools in the near future.

must always be approved by H M. Inspector. In the planning of it skill, intimate knowledge and forethought are necessary if it is to work with the minimum of friction and thus economise both time and energy The Time Table is the second school clock on the face of which are shown at intervals the hour of the day, the kind of lesson in progress in every class, the recreation interval and the moments for assembly and dismissal Its motive power is the spirit of the organiser pervading every part of the building, working silently and governing all the material changes that are necessary to a school's daily life

In framing or planning the Time Table the following additional considerations to those already named in relation to curricula should have then due weight :—

(1) The desirable amount of time to be devoted to each subject in the curriculum

(2) The desirable length of each lesson having regard to (a) the importance and difficulty of the subject, (b) whether the lesson is theoretical or practical, (c) the age of the scholars This has been already mentioned, but it is so important that attention is called to it again.

(3) The proper distribution of the lessons in relation to (a) morning or afternoon, or early and remote parts of these sessions[1]; (b) the character of the subject— whether it is chiefly mental or chiefly mechanical in its demands; (c) the staff—the strain on a teacher being great if two or three oral lessons succeed one another, (d) the internal structure of the building This point becomes accentuated if more than one teacher be working independently in the same room Quiet lessons should alternate with aggressive or noisy ones in the case of adjoining classes.

[1] See Child Study Reports in connection with the Chicago Public Schools.

In regard to 3 (a) it is an accepted view that mental power wanes under the influence of strain or fatigue. The morning therefore is better than the afternoon, and the earlier part of these sessions is better than the remoter parts, for subjects that especially demand mental vigour. Mechanical subjects such as writing, drawing, etc., are therefore usually taught in the afternoon. " Extreme fatigue lowers the *memory* power " [1]

Enlargement upon the other items set out above is prohibited by the modest proportions of this volume. The intelligent student or teacher will be able to read between the lines for himself.

The curriculum and time table having been respectively settled and arranged on a fitting basis, the teachers should remember that the mere letter of these will breed dead monotony, but that the spirit will confer life. They should further bear in mind, with regard to the scholars, this imperative dictum, " With all thy getting, get understanding ' Professor Armstrong in an address before the British Association at Belfast in 1902 said substantially the same thing : " We recognise the 3 R's in primary education, but there is need for 4 R's, the fourth being the development of reasoning power in the scholar "[2]

The time tables submitted here, as abstracts, have been found to work well. With slight modifications to meet local circumstances and needs, it is hoped they will serve the purpose of any ordinary elementary school. With the aid of the points recommended for the guidance of those planning time tables, the abstracts ought to enable any one to draw up a satisfactory working arrangement

[1] See Child Study Reports in connection with the Chicago Public Schools
[2] See Preface to the Mosely Education Commission Reports, 1904.

The following extract from the Elementary Education Act 1870 [section 7 (2)] should be carefully noted —

"The time or times during which any religious observance is practised, or instruction in religious subjects is given at any meeting of the school, shall be either at the beginning or at the end, or at the beginning and the end, of such meeting, and shall be inserted in a time table to be approved by the Education Department [now Board of Education] and *to be kept permanently and conspicuously affixed in every schoolroom* and *any scholar may be withdrawn from such observance or instruction* without forfeiting any of the other benefits of the school"

Further, in determining what shall be the curriculum and time table, the quantity of work to be accomplished should only be considered in relation to its quality   In other words, the organiser should ask himself not how much the scholars can learn in a given time, but how much they can assimilate   " The creation of a right taste , occupation of the hands and minds of children in useful ways which stimulate to industry or to directions which appeal to their love of beauty or of use ; the development of the sense of wonder at, and sympathy with, nature,— a first ingredient of worship , the encouragement of reverence for the beautiful, the good, the true,— a natural basis for religion , these are some of the ends which are kept in view when choice has to be made of subjects to companion the three R's in the school courses."[1]

And again, in regard to limitations of the curriculum " You might read all the books in the British Museum . . . and remain an utterly illiterate, uneducated person   but if you read ten pages of a good book, letter by letter,—that is to say with real accuracy, you are for ever more, in some

[1] Mr. H. T. Mark on " Moral Education in American Schools "— Special Reports, Vol 10.

measure, an educated person. The entire difference between education and non-education (as regards the merely intellectual part of it) consists in this accuracy.'[1]

TIME TABLE.—INFANTS' DEPARTMENT.

Six Classes.

SUBJECT	GRADE I	GRADE II, B	GRADE II, A	GRADE III A & B	STANDARD I
	hrs m	hrs m	hrs m	hrs m	hrs m
Scripture	3 5	3 5	3 5	3 5	3 5
					Boys Boys
Reading	1 0	2 30	2 30	2 20 25	2 30 25
Writing	—	2 0	2 0	2 0	2 10
Arithmetic (or Number)	1 0	2 20	2 50	2 50	3 5
Varied Occupations	5 0	2 0	1 0	1 30	1 30
Singing	50	1 30	1 50	1 20	1 40
Oral Lessons	1 25	1 30	1 0	1 0	1 0
				Boys	
General Intelligence and Story	1 10	30	15	30 20	30 20
Recitation	1 30	55	1 10	55	1 10
Physical Exercises	1 0	1 30	1 30	1 30	1 30
Kindergarten Games	2 10	55	30	30	30
Word building & Sentence making	—	20	30	40	1 30
Drawing	1 50	1 20	1 15	90	90
Needlework (Girls)	—	—	—	2 15	2 15
Prayers and Dismissal	1 15	50	50	50	50
Recreation	2 30	2 30	2 30	2 30	2 30
					30 Dismissal Friday.
Registration	1 15	1 15	1 15	1 15	1 15
Totals	25 00	25 00	25 00	25 00	27 30

Five minutes' play or physical exercises between each lesson

Length of lessons is half an hour in Grades I. to III. This is probably too long for the younger children.

The figures under *Boys* in the last two columns represent the additional time in minutes given by the boys only to those subjects against which the figures stand. Note that the figures in question for each of the two columns represent 2 hrs 15 mins., the time given by the girls to needlework.

---

[1] Ruskin, *Sesame and Lilies*,

Six Classes

	GRADE I.	GRADE I.	GRADE II	GRADE III.	GRADE III	STAND. I
Registration and Assembly in Hall, Morning / Registration and Preparation of Materials, Afternoon	2 30	2 30	2 30	2 30	2 30	2 30
Dressing, Assembly In Hall and Dismissal	75	75	75	50	50	50
Prayers and Hymns in Hall, Morning	50	50	50	50	5C	50
Scripture Lessons	1 40	1 40	1 40	1 40	1 40	1 40
Care of Natural Objects and Room Duties	1 30	1 30	1 30	1 55	1 40	1 40
Nature and Conversational Lessons	1 65	2 30	1 00	1 00	1 00	1 00
Kindergarten Occupations	8 45	8 20	4 05	4 40	2 40	2 50
Games in Hall	2 05	1 45	50	50	50	1 00
Finger Plays	20	20	—	—	—	—
Stories and Pictures	20	30	1 00	30	35	50
Recitation	20	30	20	25	35	History 55
Marching and Drill	1 15	1 15	1 15	1 15	1 15	1 15
Recreation	2 05	2 05	2 05	2 05	2 05	2 05
Reading and Drawing	—	—	2 30	2 30	2 20	2 30
Printing and Writing	—	—	1 15	1 15	1 40	1 40
Number	—	—	2 05	2 20	1 55	1 55
Singing	—	—	50	25	25	1 25
Needlework (Girls) / Drawing (Boys)	—	—	—	—	2 00	2 00
Home Lore and Modelling	—	—	—	—	—	35
Total Number of Hours	25 00	25 00	25 00	25 00	25 00	27 30

NOTES

1. A finger play or song at the beginning or end of each lesson
2. Five to ten minutes at the end of the long afternoon lessons to be left to the children for free use of the material in hand.
3. Groups of children—toys in a separate room under the care of a teacher.
4. Groups of children for **Gardening** under care of head or some other teacher at least **forty-five minutes** a week, according to weather.
5. Groups of children for **walks** with a teacher to Greenwich Park, etc., for Home Lore and Nature Lessons.
6. Individual children—lunch-room duties each day.

Approximately—
Grade I represents children who will be four years old at the close of the educational year
Grade II represents children who will be five years old at the close of the educational year.
Grade III represents children who will be six years old at the close of the educational year.
Standard I represents children who will be seven years old at the close of the educational year.

Time Table of a Mixed School of Twelve Classes.

Subject	Standard I		St. II	St. III	St. IV	Standard V		St. VI	St. VII	Ex-St. VII	
Scripture	$3\frac{1}{4}$	$(3\frac{1}{4}$				$3\frac{1}{4}$	$(3\frac{1}{4})$			$3\frac{1}{4}$	$(2\frac{2}{3})$
Reading	$3\frac{1}{2}$	$(3\frac{1}{2}$				2	(2)			$1\frac{1}{2}$	$(1\frac{1}{2})$
English (R., H.W., S., C., L.)	$6\frac{1}{12}$	$(5\frac{1}{12})$				$5\frac{1}{4}$	(4)			$5\frac{1}{2}$	$(5\frac{1}{2})$
Arithmetic	$5\frac{1}{4}$	(5)				$4\frac{1}{2}$	$(4\frac{1}{2})$			$4\frac{3}{4}$	$(3\frac{1}{2})$
Geography and History	1	(1)				2	(2)			2	(2)
Science	1	(1)	The same			1	(1)	As for		1	(1)
Drawing	2	$(\frac{3}{4})$	as for			2	$(\frac{3}{4})$	St. V		2	$(\frac{3}{4})$
Music	1	(1)	St. I			1	(1)			1	(1)
Physical Exercises	1	(1)				1	(1)			1	(1)
Laundry and Cookery	—	—				—	$(2\frac{1}{12})$			—	$(2\frac{3}{4})$
Manual Training	—	—				$2\frac{1}{12}$	—			$2\frac{1}{12}$	—
Needlework	—	$(2\frac{1}{2})$				—	$(2\frac{1}{2})$			—	$(2\frac{1}{2})$
Registration	$\frac{5}{6}$	$(\frac{5}{6})$				$\frac{5}{6}$	$(\frac{5}{6})$			$\frac{5}{6}$	$(\frac{5}{6})$
Recreation	$2\frac{1}{2}$	$(2\frac{1}{2})$				$2\frac{1}{2}$	$(2\frac{1}{2})$			$2\frac{1}{2}$	$(2\frac{1}{2})$
Total	$27\frac{1}{2}$	$(27\frac{1}{2}$				$27\frac{1}{2}$	$(27\frac{1}{2}$			$27\frac{1}{2}$	$(27\frac{1}{2})$

Time Table of a Berlin School of Eight Classes

Subject	Hours for Each Class per Week							
	Lowest						Highest	
	VIII	VII	VI	V	IV	III	II	I
Religion	3	3	3	4	4	6	4	4
German	8	7	7	6	6	4	6	6
Observation	2	2	2	—	—	—	—	—
History	—	—	—	2	2	2	2	3 (2)
Arithmetic	4	4	4	4	4	4	4 (2	4 (2)
Geometry	—	—	—	—	—	3	3 (2)	3 (2)
Nature Knowledge	—	—	—	2	2	4	4 (3)	3
Geography	—	—	—	2	2	2	2	2
Drawing	—	1	2 (1)	2	2	2	2	2
Writing	—	2	2	2	2	1	1	1
Singing	1	1	2	2	2	2	2	2
Gymnastics	2	2	2 (1)	2	2	2	2	2
Sewing	—	—	(2)	(2)	(2)	(3)	(4)	(4)
Total	20	22	24	28	28	32	32	32

N.B.—The numbers within brackets are for Girls

Annual Conferences,[1] as well as occasional ones to meet
urgent cases, are desirable between the head teachers of the
departments of a school with the view of (1) co-ordinating
the methods of instruction in such subjects as arithmetic,
drawing and writing; (2) arranging the time for the
recreation interval of each department so as to cause the
minimum amount of inconvenience to the other departments; (3) having a common policy in the endeavour to
bring the home and the school into harmony; (4) making
provision for the interchange of visits between the assistant
teachers of the infant and senior departments during school
hours, and (5) settling, as far as practicable, all inter-
departmental relations.

All these matters need careful re-adjustment from time
to time.

The co-ordination of methods in certain subjects is extremely important. If this is not done the progress of the
scholars will be generally retarded, and some of the
energies of the teachers wasted in every part of the school.
The methods therefore ought to be arranged by general
consent, and those adopted for subjects common to departments carried out in all loyalty. Writing especially often
suffers through the want of a general agreement on main
principles. In arithmetic, again, it is not uncommon to
find divergent ideas prevailing in different places as to the
way in which it should be taught.

As the views and influence of the assistant staff count in
these matters, the interchange of visits has been suggested,
not however entirely on this ground. Generally speaking
there is no bond of sympathy existing between the teachers
of infant and senior departments. Indeed it is not unusual
to find some teachers of senior departments openly ex-
pressing their disapproval of infant methods and infant

[1] Enforced in L.C.C. schools—Art. 64 L.C.C. S.M. Code

ways and means generally, and occasionally there is the
suggestion of a want of proper preparation for the senior
departments. This, it is submitted, is the result of a wrong
conception of the functions of an infant school on the part
of those not connected with it. In the same manner,
infant teachers perhaps do not always appreciate the difficulties of other departments—difficulties especially felt in
the lowest grades or classes. Hence the desirability for
mutual understanding and intimate individual co-operation.
If an infants' teacher is allowed to spend an occasional hour
in watching the methods and work of the senior departments and *vice versa*, it is claimed that a better correlation
of work would result, that many existing difficulties would
silently disappear, and that a clearer mental vision as to
the functions and relations of all departments would come
to every member of the staff.[1]

It is best to hold these conferences two or three months
before the close of each educational year, and to keep a
permanent record of the minutes.

[1] See pp. 2 and 135, Mosely Education Committee Reports 1904 for
similar arrangements.

CHAPTER III.

ORGANISATION IN CONNECTION WITH DISTRICT ADMINISTRATION.

Need of exceptional treatment of children in two directions.— the talented scholar ; the defective or backward scholar

THE classification of children in school departments is mainly based on the capabilities and attainments of the average scholar, but every-day experience points to the desirability or necessity of differentiating him from the talented child on the one side, and from the defective scholar on the other. Defective children may be defined as those who show a pronounced inability to learn under the ordinary conditions of school life.

Definite and extended arrangements—extended, that is, beyond the regular department—for the talented child, as a rule, only come into operation when he has reached the upper classes in the ordinary school. He can then generally be drafted to the superior primary school either by examination or nomination, according to the practice of the district, or through the agency of a scholarship secure admission to a secondary school.

On the other hand, the defective scholar needs to be specially catered for in the earlier stages of his training. He is generally so far behind the normal child in both physical and mental development that he not only falls hopelessly in the rear when educationally associated with children of average power, but otherwise suffers because—

to use a Spencerian phrase—he is altogether out of correspondence with ordinary school environment. Moreover, a feeble-minded child occasionally displays such moral depravity in the form of spitefulness, cruelty or perverted affection as may become a source of danger to others unless watchfully governed and supervised. It has therefore been considered necessary, both in the child's interests and from motives of State policy, to make special provision for his education. It has been found that about one per cent of the children attending elementary schools belongs to this defective type. The interdependence of mental power and physical development is now generally admitted, experience showing that where the former is weak there is a corresponding arrest in natural physical growth. In the same way it has been found by experiment that physical superiority in childhood gives greater vital capacity and mental grip. Moreover, "actual tests of the memory power show that the larger and stronger pupils are superior in native force of memory to the smaller and weaker. The true explanation will probably be found in the fact that those conditions which bring about large growth are favourable to the perfect formation and ideal balance of the brain and vital organs." [1]

Germany was the pioneer in this enterprise of special classes for defective children. The late London School Board, appreciating the value of the unique training in the Helfsschule, was the first educational authority in this country to establish similar classes. This was done in 1892. The movement in 1899 received State recognition by the Defective and Epileptic Children Act, and led the way to the formation of such classes in other large towns of England as well as in the United States.

[1] See Child Study Report No 3 in connection with the Chicago Public Schools.

On the other hand, the broader obligations imposed on
educational authorities recently created by the Education
Acts place within the limits of their power and administration, under certain conditions, the establishment and
supervision of secondary schools, which have long needed
to be placed on a sound organised basis The new regulations[1] for these schools issued by the Board of Education
will materially assist in this direction   Therein a secondary
school is defined as "a Day or Boarding School which
offers to each of its scholars, up to and beyond the age of
sixteen, a general education, physical, mental and moral,
given through a complete graded course of instruction, of
wider scope and more advanced degree than that given
in Elementary Schools."

The wider educational range of district administration
will enable the local authority to co-ordinate the work of
education in all its branches—to see that the primary meets
the secondary school at the right point, so that the passage
from one to the other may be rendered reasonably easy,
and to ensure that the earlier struggles of ex-elementary
scholars in the secondary school may not be so arduous as
to discourage them from continuing the course   This can
probably be best effected by the "accrediting" system
modified from American practice, and by the introduction
in the higher classes of the elementary school of some of
the studies that are taken in the lower forms of the
secondary school.

The American Ladder.

The golden ladder that enables the poorest American
child to ascend through the various educational stages and

---

[1] These further state (1) that the instruction must cover a four
years' course, and (2) that the average age of scholars commencing the
course must not be less than thirteen.

finally reach the university has many of its rungs missing
in this country Those however who ascend the ladder
here manage to negotiate the gaps, which act as deterrents
to most young aspirants.

To illustrate the American ladder it is well to indicate
roughly the various steps that may be considered to be
open to every boy and girl in the United States —

(1) The kindergarten, for children between four and six
    years of age.
(2) The elementary school, for children between six and
    fourteen years of age
(3) The high school, for children between fourteen and
    eighteen years of age
(4) The college or university, for persons between eighteen
    and twenty-two years of age
(5) The post-graduate course for persons between twenty-
    two and twenty-six years of age

The kindergarten schools have not long been established
Attendance at them is generally voluntary, but the demand
for admission is so great that buildings cannot be established fast enough to adequately meet it It may be said—
though the compulsory law varies in different States—that,
as a rule, the elementary school represents the only compulsory form of American education, the highest upward
limit of age being sixteen for enforced attendance, while
most of the States make the upward limit fourteen.

Having "graduated," or passed through the complete
course of the elementary school, the American child may
then go to the high school for a four years' course of
instruction, which is usually finished at the age of eighteen
or nineteen, though he may remain there, as a rule, until
twenty-one if unable to complete the course before Having
finished this course he is said to have "graduated ' at the

high school, and receives a certificate to that effect He is then at liberty to enter college and obtain an academic degree, which is usually conferred, not on the results of an examination, but rather on the student's record of successful work during the various college terms.

The post-graduate course, which comprises technical instruction of a highly specialised character, not easily within the range of everyone, is taken in connection with one of the many professional schools of the university Some students take this course between the ages of eighteen and twenty-two, when the ordinary academic course has been omitted

This then is substantially the American educational staircase that leads to the hall of culture and professional or technical skill. The ways and means must now be briefly recorded As each State makes its own laws there are necessarily some variations in the educational system Free education is, however, general up to eighteen years of age In some States it is free up to twenty-one years, and even practically beyond that. Attendance at all schools other than elementary is purely voluntary, but in order to go forward and upward, the student must have "graduated" or completed each preceding course Even the college or university training is free in the Western " State " universities, and nearly free elsewhere

Though the primary schools are "end on" to the high schools, the point of juncture is not quite satisfactory to the Americans themselves On the other hand, the connecting link between the high schools and the colleges or universities is both sound and strong. In the former case, something is being done in the way of introducing into the higher classes of the elementary school a few of the subjects taught in the secondary school, and by a system of conferences and interchanges of visits between the teachers of these two kinds of schools.[1] As to the relations between the high schools and the colleges, a system of nomination or "accrediting" is widely adopted, with eminently beneficial results. Some of the universities, however, still exact an entrance examination.

The "accrediting" system consists in attaching a certain number of high schools to the university in order that they may act as contributory schools. For this purpose university professors pay visits of inspection to the high schools at various times, with the view of testing their methods and general efficiency. Schools approved on the basis of these visits are accredited to the university, with the result that local nomination of the high school graduates is accepted by the university in lieu of examination. In this way the ideals in the highest seats of learning are brought into contact with the secondary schools, which in their turn might well be in similar touch with the elementary schools.

Scholarships, more limited in America than in this country, and confined practically to the universities, are also mostly awarded on a nomination basis. They are either directly awarded on the results of enquiry into the needs, character and ability of a candidate, or the university attaches a few scholarships to each of its "accredited" high schools, and allows those in authority over such schools to select their own nominees.

The whole system of educational organisation in America is therefore a great contrast to that in England, where a gulf intervenes between the elementary and the secondary school, and between the latter and the university, soon probably to be filled up or bridged over. The scholarship schemes just adopted (Feb 1905) by the London County Council will probably help in this direction. The recent

[1] See Mr. W. C. Fletcher's report, Mosely Education Commission.

action too of the Board of Education[1] in setting the
standard and limitations for the secondary schools, and in
grading them on fresh lines, seems to point to a new
educational era The Board is clearly feeling its way,[2]
evidently intending at present to leave as large a measure
of initiative as possible with the local education authority,
now endowed with such wide and far-reaching powers

It is hoped that, following the American practice, a
combined system of "graduation" and nomination will
soon be allowed to take the place of examination in the
passage from one grade of school to another.

Higher Grade Schools

Something has already been accomplished in England
in the way of bringing elementary school aims nearer to
those associated with the better class secondary school.
This has been brought about by the establishment of the
higher grade and, later, the "higher elementary" school

The higher grade schools have not, in many cases, had a
proper opportunity of fulfilling their mission Instead of
making these schools what their name implied, some of the
late school boards, treading on uncertain ground, were
content, as a rule, to take one or two senior departments of
an ordinary school and convert them into higher grade
departments without removing the lower standards It is
common now, in some areas, to find Standards II. to IV.
in these higher grade schools It was thus a conversion
more in name than in reality

Contributory schools were, of course, attached to these
converted departments, the working hours of which were

[1] See Regulations for Secondary Schools, 1904
[2] "Much of the work that has to be done in establishing a general
system of secondary schools is experimental."—Prefatory Memorandum
to Secondary School Regulations, 1904.

slightly extended for the uppermost classes, and highly
qualified teachers were appointed to give instruction to the
senior scholars As far as possible also a laboratory and
art room were added

One of the first difficulties that higher grade departments had to face was the apathy and in some instances
the opposition of the contributory schools, inasmuch as the
latter were threatened with the loss of their upper standards,
or the best scholars in them This strained relationship
would probably not have arisen had the higher grade
schools been put, in the first place, on a sound footing, viz.,
by confining the education given therein solely to the
elder and more advanced boys and girls, and by giving to
higher grade departments an independent existence distinct
from the organisation of any other department. It thus
happened that often only a scanty and reluctant supply of
upper standard children came from the neighbouring or
contributory schools Instead, therefore, of finding much
larger upper classes in the higher grade departments, as
was intended by this arrangement, it sometimes happened
that an ordinary school was as well, if not better off, in
this respect than some higher grade departments.

Many higher grade schools, however, more successful
than others, but established under similar or the same
conditions as those already indicated, having secured large
upper classes and being able to do more advanced work
than the ordinary schools, were nevertheless generally
hampered with administrative difficulties inherent to their
peculiar constitution. These were—

(1) All the children educated on the premises of a
higher grade school—in the junior departments and in the
lower standards of the higher grade department itself—had
the right, without any principle of selection, to pass, step
by step, or class by class, into the upper standards, where

the talented or advanced scholars from the contributory
schools were also taught. This mixture of talent with
mediocrity was not conducive to progress, and was contrary
to the main principle underlying the establishment of
superior primary schools.

(2) Success in obtaining many scholars from the contributory schools cramped the flow of promotion from the
junior departments on the same premises as the higher
grade school, since no department may admit more children
than it can officially accommodate

(3) Even in the most favourable case of the type of a
higher grade school now being discussed, viz., where four
departments existed—the infants', the junior mixed
(Standards I to IV.), the girls' higher grade (Standard V
and upwards), the boys' higher grade (Standard V and
upwards)—grave difficulties were encountered It occasionally happened that the higher grade departments could
not receive the full annual draft of scholars from the
junior mixed department, which in turn could not therefore receive the full draft from the infants', thus causing
an unfortunate block

On the other hand, if to avoid the difficulty it is arranged
to select only the more advanced scholars in Standard IV
of the junior mixed department for promotion to the higher
grade school, then the remaining scholars of that standard
would necessarily have to leave the school with which they
had been probably associated since infancy and go to
another school

Thus it is that the higher grade schools built up on the
conditions named here have been seriously hampered.
Those, however, which started with an independent existence and gave exclusive attention to the upper standards
have, as a rule, been an unqualified success. If higher
grade schools are to continue as one of the crowning points

of primary education, the following conditions are essential —

(1) That each higher grade school must have an independent existence and be complete in itself, *i.e.*, it must not form part of an ordinary school, and no particular department or school should have a special claim upon its accommodation.

(2) That the higher grade school should receive no children above twelve years of age, or below full Standard IV attainments.

(3) That, as a rule, only those should be admitted to the higher grade course who show commendable industry and more than average talent [1]

The advantages of higher grade schools of the best type are —

(1) It is an incentive to industry for scholars in the ordinary school to know that successful devotion to work will enable them later to go to a school of higher status and more advanced instruction.

(2) Scholars of ability are able to advance more rapidly when they are better classified, have more skilful teachers and are not retarded by the presence of children possessing average or below average capabilities.

(3) The higher grade school increases a child's opportunities of obtaining a scholarship and thus passing on to a secondary school. It also improves his outlook and widens his view.

(4) Generally, the superior tone of a higher grade school, arising chiefly from the mutually stimulating effect of the stronger moral power possessed by scholars of firm mental calibre and previously recognised good conduct, is a most valuable force in forming character. These scholars

---

[1] Exceptions to this are desirable in poor districts.—*Vide* p 108.

must in turn influence others of their own social status
with whom they are brought into contact

(5) The higher grade department is a fitting transition
school for those going later to secondary schools

The higher grade school as considered here must not
be confounded with the " Higher Elementary " which has
official recognition as part of the elementary school system

The Higher Elementary School.

A higher elementary school,[1] limited generally to 350
pupils, must be recognised by the Board of Education as
such, and the curriculum and time table must also be
approved by the same central authority. The school must
be organised to give a complete four years' course of
graduated instruction Other main conditions of recognition are (1) a sufficiency of science instruction, both
practical and theoretical, for each year s course; (2) special
equipment for practical instruction, (3) H M. Inspector
must be satisfied that each scholar is qualified to profit by
the kind of instruction offered ; (4) each scholar must, as
a rule, commence with the first year's course and proceed
upward year by year, (5) the number of scholars in a class
should not generally exceed 35 and must not exceed 40

The curriculum of a higher elementary school should
be, in the fitting words of Mr. Morant in discussing the
" French system of higher primary schools,"[2] " at once
more limited in duration than that of the secondary
school, more capable of assimilation by children of ex-
elementary attainments, and more immediately applicable
to actual use at the desk, the counter, or the workshop,
to which the great mass of the scholars are inevitably
bound to go at as early an age as fifteen or sixteen "

[1] See Arts. 38-42, Code 1901.   [2] See Special Reports, Vol. 1

The local authority, subject to condition (3) above, determines what shall be the means of admission to a higher elementary school   The practice, therefore, in this respect varies a little   In London the regular primary schools within reasonable distance are annually invited to nominate scholars for the neighbouring higher elementary school.   These nominations, as a rule, greatly exceed the number of vacancies   An examination is therefore held and the most suitable children selected for admission, the parents giving a guarantee that their children will remain at school to complete the four years' course

A similar promise is usually exacted from parents when children are admitted from contributory schools to a higher grade department

It is obvious, since the age and time limitation for each scholar in the higher elementary school is the close of the educational year in which he attains the age of fifteen, that each child must secure admission when not more than eleven years old, otherwise the conditional four years' course of instruction could not be completed   It thus happens that most of the children admitted to a higher elementary school are those who have just fully reached Standard IV. attainments.   The contributory schools therefore are not truncated in this instance, but retain their upper classes almost intact, minus a few talented children   As the higher elementary schools generally draw their pupils from a wider field than the higher grade schools, the contributory schools in the former case do not feel that the drain on their talent is so exhaustive as in the latter case

The advantages previously attributed to education in the higher grade schools apply with even greater force to the higher elementary school   The aims of both these schools and the serviceable work they have done may be gathered from the following statement issued in a memo-

randum by the London Association of Head Teachers of
Higher Grade Schools, 1904 —

"A large number of children have obtained the London
County Council minor scholarships A few have gained
intermediate London County Council scholarships, while
many have passed the preliminary stage of that examination A very large number have passed the Oxford and
Cambridge Junior Local Examinations (some in the
Honours Divisions), the Chamber of Commerce and other
higher examinations, for the preparation of which there
would have been little opportunity in the contributory
schools And not the least advantage gained by transfer
to the higher grade school has been the extended school
life of many of the children

"The following comparative table of results of the
Oxford Local Examinations in July, 1904, is of importance
in connection with the advantages of higher grade
schools —

	Total number of can-didates	No of over age candi-dates	Percen-tage of candi-dates obtain-ing a certifi-cate	Percen-tage of candi-dates obtain-ing honours	No of distinc-tions ob tained
OXFORD SENIOR LOCAL					
From the whole country	3200	702	62 9	13 7	277
,, London Secondary Schools	339	64	65 8	6 2	12
,, L C C Higher Grade and H E Schools ..	32	0	93 7	18 7	3
OXFORD JUNIOR LOCAL					
From the whole country	6720	1500	67 6	18 2	385
,, London Secondary Schools	602	157	65 5	13 3	21
,, L C C Higher Grade, etc	640	21	80 6	27 2	34

Some differences between the higher grade and the

higher elementary school have been already noted   Other differences are :

(1) The higher elementary schools may only admit scholars once a year and only through the one recognised channel   whereas the higher grade schools may, as a rule, admit suitable children at any period of the year provided there is accommodation,

(2) The higher elementary schools whose constitution is governed by the Board of Education are much the same in character throughout the country   whereas the higher grade schools vary more or less in constitution according to the educational areas in which they are situated

(3) In a higher elementary school a scholar must take each year's course in succession   In the higher grade schools there is nothing to prevent a scholar being promoted over two classes in one year, though each class may generally represent a year's work

There appears to be no doubt that the higher elementary department is a more satisfactory form of superior primary school than the higher grade department   It is probable, however, that the latter form may prove the more suitable in very poor districts, in which children almost invariably leave school at the earliest legal opportunity, and in which the number of scholars in the upper standards of each school is generally small   It would therefore be a gain in this instance to have a higher grade department into which the whole of the scholars in Standard VI or VII and upwards could be drafted   If only a two years' course could be secured in a higher grade department in this way, with the opportunity thus afforded for sound classification, it would probably prove extremely valuable to the children concerned.

The following are abstracts of working time tables for higher grade and higher elementary schools —

HIGHER GRADE SCHOOL.

(Separate Departments for Boys and Girls.)

	Std. III.	Std. IV.	Std. V.	Std. VI.	Std. VII.	Ex. (C).	Ex. (B).	Ex. (A).
Scripture	2½ (2½)	2½ (2½)	2½ (2½)	2 (2½)	2 (2½)	2½ ( )	2½ (2½)	2½ (2½)
Mathematics	3¾ (3¾)	3¾ (3¾)	6 (4¾)	4½ (4¾)	6 (5¼)	4¼ ( )	5½ (6½)	4½ (5¾)
English	6¼ ($3\frac{7}{12}$)	4½ ($3\frac{8}{12}$)	4½ (4)	4½ (4)	2¾ (3¾)	4 ( )	5¼ (5¼)	3½ (5¼)
Reading	2½ (3½)	2 (2)	1½ (2¼)	1¼ (2¼)	¾ (1½)	— ( )	— (—)	— (—)
Writing	1½ (1½)	1 (1½)	¾ (½)	¾ (½)	½ (—)	— ( )	— (—)	— (—)
French	— (—)	2¼ (1½)	1¾ (3)	2¼ (3)	3¼ (2¾)	3¾ ( )	2¼ (2¾)	2¼ (2¾)
Science { Practical	— (—)	— (—)	— (—)	— (—)	¾ (—)	2 ( )	2 (—)	2¾ (—)
Science { Theoretical.. ..	1½ (1½)	1½ (1)	1½ (1¾)	1½ (1¾)	1½ (2)	1 ( )	¾ (2½)	3 (2½)
Geography	2¼ (1)	3¼ (1)	2¼ (1¼)	2¼ (1¼)	1½ (1¾)	1¼ ( )	1¾ (2)	1 (2)
History	— (1)	— (1)	1½ (1¼)	1½ (1¼)	1½ (1½)	2¼ ( )	1¾ (1¾)	1½ (1¾)
Drawing	2¼ (1)	2¼ (1)	2¾ (1)	2¼ (1)	2¼ (2)	2¼ ( )	2 (2)	2¾ (2¾)
Singing	1 ($1\frac{2}{12}$)	1 ($1\frac{2}{12}$)	1½ (1½)	1 (1½)	½ (¾)	— ( )	— (¾)	— (¾)
Manual Training	— (—)	— (—)	—† (—)	2¾ (—)	2¼ (—)	2¾ ( )	2¾ (—)	2¾ (—)
Physical Exercises	1 (1)	1 (1)	1 (1)	1 (1)	1 (1)	1 ( )	1 (1)	1 (1)
Optional Lesson	($\frac{7}{12}$)	($\frac{7}{12}$)	(½)	(½)	(½)	( )	(½)	(½)
Needlework	— (2½)	— (2½)	— (2¼)	— (2¼)	— (2¼)	— ( )	— (—)	— —
Registration	— (—)	— (—)	— (—)	— (—)	— (—)	— ( )	— (—)	— (—
Recreation	3 ($2\frac{1}{12}$)	2½ ($2\frac{1}{12}$)	2½ (2½)	2½ (2½)	2½ (2½)	2½ ( )	2½ (2½)	2½ (2½
Totals	27½ (26¼) *	27½ (27¼) *	30 (30)	30 (30)	30 (30)	30 ( )	30 (30)	30 (30

Cookery and Laundry Classes formed from V., VI., and VI. (B) respectively, but not complete class attending at any one time.

* Time table ceases at 4.15 p.m.; optional work 4.15 to 4.30: 26¼ + 1¼ = 27½.

† A small proportion of Standard V. take Manual Training. This proportion increases as the school year advances. The time thus occupied is mainly at the expense of Mathematics and English.

HIGHER ELEMENTARY SCHOOL (BOYS')

CLASSES	1st Year's Course		2nd Year's Course		3rd Year's Course		4th Year's Course	
	h	m	h	m	h	m	h	m
English	6	0	6	5	4	10	4	5
History	1	0	1	0	1	0	1	5
Geography	1	0	1	0	1	0	1	0
French	2	15	2	15	2	50	3	0
Singing	1	0	1	0	1	0	1	0
Physical Exercise	1	0	1	0	1	0	1	0
Mathematics	5	15	5	40	5	10	5	0
Physics, Theoretical				40	1	0	1	0
,, Practical			1	20	2	0	2	0
Chemistry, Theoretical				40	1	0	1	0
,, Practical			1	20	2	0	2	0
Science : Experimental Geometry & Mensuration	1	0						
Art	1	30	1	30	1	20	1	20
Geometry		15		15		15		15
Woodwork	2	5	2	5				
Metalwork					2	5	2	5
Recreation	1	10	1	10	1	10	1	10
Scripture	2	30	2	0	2	0	2	0
TOTAL HOURS PER WEEK	30	0	30	0	30	0	30	0

TIME TABLE¹ OF A HIGHER ELEMENTARY PRUSSIAN
SCHOOL (BOYS').

SUBJECTS OF INSTRUCTION	NUMBER OF WEEKLY HOURS					
	Highest)			Lowest)		
	I.	II.	III.	IV.	V.	VI.
Religion	2	2	2	3	3	3
German, incl. Reading and Writing	4	6	8	12	12	12
Arithmetic	3	3	3	5	5	5
Elements of Geometry	3	2	2	—	—	—
Natural Science	2	2	2	—	—	—
Physics (Chemistry)	3	2	—	—	—	—
Geography	2	2	2	2	—	—
History	2	2	2	—	—	—
French (or English)	5	5	5	—	—	—
Drawing	2	2	2	2	—	—
Singing	2	2	2	2	2	2
Gymnastics	2	2	2	2	2	2
Total	32	32	32	28	24	24

¹ See *History and Organisation of Public Education in the German Empire*, by Dr. Lexis.

The superior primary schools of Germany are similar to the higher grade type (not the higher elementary) in this country, inasmuch as the lower classes merely represent the ordinary primary school. In France, however, the *Ecoles primaires supérieures*[1] are built somewhat on the lines of the higher elementary here. A pupil of the regular elementary school, having obtained the *certificat d'études* (leaving certificate), can go to the superior primary school for a three years' course of instruction. During the first year the instruction is of a *general* character, but for the second and third year pupils the curriculum is divided into three sections or courses, to any one of which the pupil must give his exclusive attention. These courses are designated (1) the Commercial, (2) the Industrial, (3) the Agricultural. Theory and practice are judiciously blended. There is no attempt to teach a business or trade. The idea is, in the closing years of school life, that a child should have an opportunity, under careful guidance, of developing his powers on the lines suitable to his particular bent.

In Holland the Burgher and Higher Burgher schools occupy an intermediate position between the regular elementary and the higher secondary schools (Gymnasia). The curricula, however, of the Higher Burgher schools are generally of a more ambitious type than that of the higher elementary schools in this country.

The Contributory School.

The Contributory school, being a regular elementary school with its seven or eight grades or standards, holds relatively to the superior primary school a position of remote subordination, inasmuch as the finer material in its upper classes is subject to requisition. The novelty of

[1] See Special Reports, Vol. 7.

this position, when first created, natually led to heart-
burnings on the part of some of the teachers of the
Contributory schools On the whole, however, they displayed a worthy public spirit by the way in which most of
the superior schools were supported, when time had
smoothed away the earlier apprehensions It was recognised that though the Contributory system had its defects,
the educational gain outweighed them many times

There can be no doubt that the child who migrates from
school to school suffers by the change in many ways, but
this does not apply to the passage of the older children
from the ordinary to the superior primary school The
means of minimising the educational loss caused chiefly
through capricious or necessary migration is one of serious
moment Various partial remedies have been suggested:
(1) The adoption of a uniform educational year for all
schools in the same district; (2) A practically uniform
curriculum for schools in the same educational area; (3) An
organised system promoted by the local education authority
to prevent capricious migration from school to school

The Continuation School.

This term, as understood here, applies to both day and
evening classes that provide for technical or general
education, or for the *continuation* of one s education, after
leaving the regular day school The whole of these
classes may be divided into (1) Day classes, (2) Evening
classes, (3) Correspondence classes

(1) *Day Classes*

The Day classes have mostly been established at
technical institutes for the use of artisans and apprentices in skilled trades, the employers co-operating with the
educational authority for this purpose In England the
general and intimate connection between the industries on

the one hand and education on the other, such as exists in America, is wanting There is, however, evidence that this country is awakening to the importance of the link, now that the Mosely Education Commission has directed so much attention to the American practice in this matter

Thus in several large towns some employers of labour are allowing such apprentices as are likely to profit by a course of technical training to attend suitable classes during the day at the technical institutes, attendance at such classes being deemed practically equivalent to attendance at the works Middlesborough, Birmingham, Swindon, and Woolwich may be cited as examples The London County Council, too, in the case of the Central School of Arts and Crafts and the Northampton Institute, allows the payment of bursaries to students at the Saturday morning classes in silversmithing and press tool making The bursaries are intended to cover loss of wages, travelling and other incidental expenses

The Woolwich Arsenal authorities have co-operated with the governors of the Polytechnic in the district in order to insure the proper technical training of lads engaged in the Royal Arsenal[1] During the first three years of apprenticeship a lad receives instruction at the Polytechnic for ten hours and a half a week, three hours in one afternoon and the rest of the time in the evenings Regularity of attendance, good conduct and sound application are insisted upon Each lad pays a small annual fee to cover instruction, cost of books, drawing outfit and paper, such fees being refunded by the Arsenal authority if attendance and progress have been satisfactory throughout the year The War Office gives a grant of £400 per annum towards

[1] See interesting paper read before the Association of Technical Institutions at Liverpool, January, 1905, by the Principal of the Woolwich Polytechnic.

the cost of instruction, and the London County Council and the Board of Education co-operate in a similar way.

The first-year lads receive instruction in mathematics, experimental science and mechanical drawing, the second-year lads take up additionally practical mechanics, heat and electricity, but dropping experimental science; while in the third year more advanced work is taken on the basis of the second year studies. Those who volunteer to continue their studies at the close of the three years' course are allowed to specialise by taking up subjects particularly adapted to their trades. In the laboratories the lads work in pairs, but each one must keep, in a book provided for the purpose, a record of the experiments made. The Principal of the Polytechnic sends weekly reports on each lad's conduct and work to the chief superintendent of the Arsenal.

In order to encourage home work and to insure it being done under favourable conditions, a room is reserved for the lads at the Polytechnic and a teacher placed in charge of it. This supervision secures quietude of study, and assistance to individual students who may stand in need of help. This work of preparation and private study is compulsory and is included in the ten hours and a half already mentioned.

The following is a brief outline of the scheme in operation at Swindon :—

Day Studentships for Apprentices at Swindon.[1]

In order to encourage apprentices to gain a sound knowledge of technical science, the G.W.R. Company offer facilities for a limited number of selected students to attend day classes at the technical school.

---

[1] Extract from the Prospectus of the Swindon Technical Institute.

The number of studentships will be limited to thirty at any one time, generally in groups as follows—for a three years' course:

1st year's course	15 students
2nd ,,	9 ,,
3rd ,,	6 ,,

For each year's course there will be a competitive examination, successful students passing on from one year's course to the next.

The course of study for each year will consist of:

Practical mathematics
Practical mechanics
Geometrical and machine drawing
Heat, electricity and chemistry

Candidates must be registered apprentices between seventeen and eighteen years of age on the 1st of June in the year of entry upon the course.

They must have spent at least one year in the factory, and must have regularly attended for at least one session the preparatory group of evening classes at the technical school.

They must produce evidence of good conduct and attention to their work in the factory and at the technical school, and only those who attain a minimum qualification at the examination will be successful.

Successful students will attend day classes at the technical school on two afternoons per week for 26 weeks, from September to April.

Those attending the classes will have their wages paid as if at work in the factory, and the G.W.R. Company will pay their school fees.

The students attending the day classes will be expected to give some time each evening to private study. They should devote themselves particularly to the prescribed course, so as to obtain a thorough knowledge of a few of the most important subjects rather than a smattering of a great number.

Students who distinguish themselves will be allowed to spend part of their last year in the drawing office or chemical laboratory.

At this same school, trade classes are held for carriage and waggon builders, boilermakers, coppersmiths, tinsmiths, electric wiremen, plumbers, and for others engaged in the building trade.

In connection with most of these classes, a fairly good general education, a careful selection of apprentices, and a periodical report (preferably a monthly one) on each student to the employer, appear very desirable.

Day classes at technical institutes are also available for those who, before assuming the responsibilities of apprenticeship, desire to go through a course of specialised instruction relating to the trade or technical profession they propose to adopt

" Such institutions afford systematic instruction in day classes in courses extending over two or more years, and adapted for the preparation of young men for employment in connection with the trades, manufactures, and commerce of the country; they also provide the higher courses of specialised instruction in science in relation to particular industries. Corresponding provision is made for advanced instruction in art in the day time, under conditions which lend themselves to the arrangement of courses of instruction aiming at the preparation of students for work connected with the applications of art to the industries." [1]

(2) *Evening Schools.*

These necessarily vary in kind according to diversity of conditions in various localities Roughly, for the larger centres of population, the evening schools may be classified under—

(1) *Ordinary schools*, meeting generally three or four times a week from 7 30 to 9 30 p.m

(2) *Commercial schools*, meeting generally five evenings a week from 7 to 10 o'clock

(3) *Science and Art schools*, meeting generally five evenings a week and on Saturday mornings

(4) *Technical Institutes and Polytechnics* Day and evening classes

(5) *Schools of Art.*   Day and evening classes.

[1] See Prefatory Memorandum to Regulations for Evening Schools, Technical Institutions, etc., 1901.

As a condition precedent to the earning of grants, these schools must conform to the Regulations of the Board of Education for evening schools, technical institutions and schools of art   These regulations have been made purposely elastic in order to enable local authorities to establish classes suitable to the economical conditions and industrial needs of the district

Students may not be registered for grant-earning purposes who are under twelve years of age, or who are earning grant under other regulations of the Board.

The organisation of evening schools is, as a rule, based entirely on subjects of instruction, each class being, as it were, a miniature school in itself   The courses of instruction are usually arranged to cover a session's work, which generally extends from September to Easter or Whitsuntide. Though each session's course is complete in itself, a series of courses in the more advanced subjects is so correlated that one session's work will easily dovetail into the next The ordinary evening school is intended principally for those who, having left the school, wish to improve their general education.   The curriculum therefore is framed on those lines, though extensions are permissible for students desiring instruction beyond the ordinary range.

The name Commercial schools suggests the subjects of instruction   They aim, of course, at such preparation as will enable the pupils to qualify for commercial life, or to enhance their value if already engaged in it.   The examination standards generally aimed at are those set by the London Chamber of Commerce, the Society of Arts, and the Senior Oxford and Cambridge Locals

The Science and Art schools generally arrange specific courses of instruction in the various sciences, etc, recognised by the Board of Education.   Laboratory or practical work supplements the theoretical lessons   No provision is

made, as a rule, for technical instruction on the lines of
trade classes

The technical institutes and schools of art, on the other
hand, generally specialise in the direction of trade classes
and in art training as applied to the industries Many
polytechnics, however, include in their curricula such
subjects as are taught in the commercial schools, and also,
in a more advanced form, many of the subjects taught at
the science and art schools.

It is interesting to note that Messrs Brunner, Mond
and Co.,[1] of Cheshire, have made it a rule not to employ
any boy unless he has passed Standard VI. and undertakes
to attend an evening school until he is 19 years of age
This firm's determination has had a salutary effect upon
other youths in the neighbourhood in the way of encouraging evening studies.

Some Continuation Schools Abroad.

In the United States manual training and trade schools
reach a high state of perfection The close relationship
between the technical institutes and the industries, and the
determination of employers to have their apprentices
thoroughly educated, make educational and industrial
progress comparatively easy. The following extract from
Alderman J R Heape's report (Mosely Education Commission) illustrates the enterprise there.

The Baldwin Locomotive Works in Philadelphia "take
apprentices at 17 for four years, who must have had 'a
good common school education'; they are required to
attend such night schools during the first three years of
their apprenticeship as will teach them, in the first year,
elementary algebra and geometry, and, in the remaining

[1] See article on Evening Continuation Schools by J. C. Medd,
School, i., 261.

two years, the rudiments of mechanical drawing. An apprentice of the second class must have had a high school training, including the mathematical courses usual in such schools. He must attend night schools for the study of mechanical drawing at least two years unless he has already sufficiently acquired the art. In Chicago the bricklayers and masons' union have for four years required a considerable basis of educational attainment from those who seek to be apprenticed at 16. It is afterwards compulsory upon them to attend a special school five days each week for three months in the year to receive a specialised instruction in mathematics, mechanical drawing, English, and the construction of language.

Free evening lectures are given in the public schools of New York. These are largely attended by adults. Discussion is encouraged, and the free libraries of the city co-operate to lend books to the auditors who desire to enter more deeply into the subject of the lecture.

In many parts of Germany[1] attendance at the evening school is compulsory from 14 to 16, or 14 to 18, years of age, unless the student has already reached a satisfactory standard of educational attainment. This compulsion is of a stern type, for the student must learn, and the employer is forced to give the time necessary for it. From the ordinary evening schools of Berlin have grown such institutions as the " Handwerkerschulen," which, as the name implies, are schools for apprentices and artisans. In many of the trade schools there are courses of instruction extending over periods from six months to four and a half years. These courses are so arranged that attendance at the lessons need not be continuous throughout the year. An artisan, for example, could attend during the winter months only, and give up the summer months

[1] See Special Reports, Vol. 9, Continuation Schools of Berlin.

to the practical work of earning a livelihood, and so complete the full course of instruction in this alternative way
The ordinary German evening schools are much the same
as those in the large towns of England

Holland shows a similar enterprise to Germany in the
establishment of trade schools with day and evening
sections, and of other continuation schools of a commercial
and general character

(3) *Correspondence Classes*,[1]

A phenomenal success has been achieved by the International Correspondence School at Scranton, U S These
classes are mainly intended for artisans and others who
from various causes are unable to attend either day or
evening schools This school, by its simple text-books on
the theory and technique of the various skilled trades and
other occupations and by careful guidance of its pupils,
has served a most useful purpose In the words of the
United States Commissioner of Labour, " there are so many
cases where the system of instruction pursued by these
schools has enabled the students to advance from the lower
branches of a trade or occupation to a complete mastery of
the same, that it would be impossible to estimate the
benefits that have accrued to those who have been under
instruction In the higher positions are to be found fore-
men, superintendents, master plumbers and builders,
architects, and electrical and mechanical engineers, who
bear witness to the worth of this instruction "

Combinations of Schools for purposes other than Co-ordination

Such combinations may be promoted directly by the
local authority or by one of its officers, or by the teachers

[1] See Mosely Education Commission Report, especially Mr. John
Whitburn's article.

of the district with that authority's sanction and approval.
Combinations due chiefly to unofficial or semi-official
enterprise are:—(1) Swimming Associations. (2) Athletic
Sports Associations. (3) Literary Societies. (4) Natu-
ralist Clubs. (5) Choral Unions. (6) Social gather-
ings, etc.

When municipal baths, the river or the sea are reasonably near and otherwise suitable for the purpose, swimming
frequently forms part of the school instruction in the
summer months, especially in the case of boys' departments. It has been found a valuable incentive both to
collective and individual effort to have a school swimming
association for the district, and for such association to
organise competitions among the schools, and to award
certificates, medals, etc , to teachers for skill, and to
scholars for progress, in the aquatic art. The work of
the London Schools' Swimming Association is an example
of what may be accomplished in this way.

In a similar manner and with equally satisfactory results,
a sports association, with its cricket and football branches,
has had its value enhanced by a district organisation. A
junior naturalists' club,[1] for either boys or girls or both,
has been found in some instances to be an effective force
in school life. Under careful direction and management
it should prove in every senior department an instrument
of great educational power

Literary or choral societies are suitable for the evening
schools combining in a given area. The choral unions of
the London evening classes have been a great success.
Each large district has formed such a union. Arrangements are made for each school to study during the session
selected pieces of classical or semi-classical music, partially
or wholly combined rehearsals taking place at intervals

---

[1] This has been tried in America with success.

Towards the close of the session a musical festival is held by the combined schools

It is suggested that two or more day schools might profitably join hands to promote simple lectures on the easier English classics for the eldest scholars An occasional " evening " with Longfellow, Tennyson, etc , would prove most effective.

Among official combinations of schools are the following —

(1) Combinations for purposes of lantern illustrations
(2)   ,,   of evening classes with day schools
(3)   ,,   for subjects taught at centres
(4)   ,,   for prize distributions
(5)   ,,   for management—local managers
(6)   ,,   for exhibitions
(7)   ,,   for examinations (scholarships, etc)
(8)   ,,   for interchange of letters between
            senior pupils.

Some of these need a word of explanation

With the view of giving effective illustration to lessons in Geography and History, the late School Board for London allowed not more than twenty senior departments to combine to form a district One central school was selected as a centre for lantern slides and books of reference A committee of the head teachers drew up courses of instruction in the two subjects, which in all material points were to apply to the schools of the district Suitable lantern slides were supplied to fit in with these courses, usually in boxes containing from ten to eighteen slides Then, by means of a scheme of rotation, every school obtained the box of slides it needed at the right time Each school was, of course, supplied with a good lantern and all accessories. This arrangement has worked well in

its limited application, and has added greatly to the interest
of the scholars in their lessons.

Association of day with evening schools has taken the
contributory form. The practice has been, in some areas,
to attach a certain number of day senior departments to
each evening school, the head teachers of the former
supplying once a quarter a list of the scholars, with
addresses, who had left the school and were no longer
under the obligation to attend. It is then the duty of the
responsible teacher of the evening school to communicate
with the ex-scholars named on the list with the view of
securing their attendance at school in the evenings.

The centre system of instruction in such subjects as
woodwork, cookery, and laundry necessitates an organised
combination of schools so that the centre may be fully
utilised and the least possible inconvenience caused to the
departments sending classes there.

With regard to the local managers, it is usual to group
three or more schools together, and place them under the
management of one local committee.

Interchange of Letters.

It is well for schools to combine for this purpose so that
each willing scholar in the upper parts of the school may
have a correspondent in some other school, no matter how
remote. In this way London may write to Edinburgh,
York to Canterbury, Birmingham to Liverpool, etc. It is
probably best, though it is not a material point, for towns
that are widely different in character to join hands in
this way, e.g. Bradford with Grimsby, Newcastle with
Nottingham, Swansea with Kidderminster, Manchester
with Plymouth, and so on.

A scheme for interchange of letters on these lines is in
operation in London schools, provided and non-provided,

except that the correspondence in this case is officially
limited to the United States and the Colonies There is
nothing, however, to prevent head teachers supplementing
this scheme by acting on their own initiative and responsibility The chief points in the London scheme are - (1) The
first letters are, as a rule, written abroad and are distri-
buted by the Education Department of the Council among
the various schools that have expressed a wish to join in the
scheme   (2) Replies are then sent either direct or through
the Education Offices, according to arrangements made by
the controlling authorities at each end (3) When the
opening letters are written in London they are forwarded
in school batches to the Education Department of the
Council, and thence transmitted to the corresponding
department abroad   After the first letter, however, communications are sent direct after being seen by the head
teachers (4) When several replies have to be sent to the
same school they are enclosed in one envelope and forwarded to the head teacher at the other end for distribution among the scholars to whom they are addressed
(5) Teachers are requested to see that the letters written
by their pupils are interesting Touches of personal
history, brief accounts of places in old or new London,
pressed flowers, pictures from illustrated papers, &c.,
coloured views of buildings in London such as are given
for Reward Cards, are suggested for purposes of
strengthening the correspondence link (6) Reward
Cards and suitable notepaper are supplied to the schools,
and teachers are refunded any expenditure incurred in
postage On these lines correspondence is carried on with
the following Colonies and States —

Bahamas Islands (boys only)	Demerara (boys only)
Barbados Islands (boys only)	Manitoba
British Columbia	New Zealand

Prince Edward Island	Michigan
Straits Settlements (boys only)	Nebraska
Tasmania	Newport, R I
Transvaal	Oklahoma
Victoria	Washington
California (boys only)	Wyoming
Connecticut	South Carolina (girls only)
Maine	Saratoga
Massachusetts	Illinois (girls only)

Half Time Schools [1]

Under provisions of the Education Acts and the bye-laws of Local Education Authorities, children may obtain partial exemption from school for purposes of employment. Such children must attend school half-time, *i e*, five times a week, and receive on each attendance two hours' secular instruction To meet the needs of these children half-time schools have been established in agricultural districts and other centres of industry As far as practicable, one set of scholars attend in the morning and another in the afternoon. " The term ' half-time scholar ' means a scholar certified by the Local Authority to be employed in conformity with the bye-laws, or, if not subject to the bye-laws, in conformity with the Elementary Education Act, 1876, or any other Act regulating the education of children employed in labour, and in either case recognised by the Board as a half-time scholar. '

The scholar must be over eleven years of age and be " beneficially and necessarily employed

Industrial Schools.

These institutions have become a necessary part of the educational system They were established to meet the special needs of children charged before a magistrate either

[1] See Revised Circular No 224, May 16, 1896   Also Art 43 (*d*), Code 1904.

under (1) the Industrial Schools Act of 1866, or (2) the Elementary Education Act of 1876 It is the duty of the magistrate, the case being satisfactorily proved, and if he considers the course a proper one, to consign the offender to one of these schools for a definite period

Truant schools are similar in character to the industrial schools, but the means of obtaining admission to the former are different from those already indicated. A child must not only be a confirmed truant, but he must also disobey a magistrate's order to attend an ordinary elementary school with reasonable regularity, before he can be committed to a truant school

Most of these institutions are residential. They are really half-time schools so far as the regular elementary school curriculum is concerned, the other five half-days being devoted to manual training in wood and metal work, tailoring, bootmaking, gardening, farming and other kindred employments of a practical nature.

Institutions of a like character are in existence in the United States and most European countries. They are called Parental Schools in America

It is, perhaps, as well to say that the offences under the two Acts of Parliament named range from "no visible means of subsistence" to any offence punishable by imprisonment.

Vacation Schools[1] are of comparatively recent growth and due chiefly to private enterprise. They are organised arrangements for giving to the children of large towns, during the summer months or summer vacation, such agreeable, practical, and partial employment of an educational character as they naturally desire to have For this purpose, a few school buildings and playgrounds, under, of

[1] See Report of the Education Commission of Chicago, 1900.

course, proper guidance and supervision, become a busy hive during the long summer holiday. Manual training and nature study are the subjects mostly taken by the boys. The girls, too, take up the latter subject together with the domestic arts and other manual exercises, while the infants are happily employed with kindergarten games.

These employments are supplemented by occasional excursions into the country. As far as possible, the work is carried on in the playground or other open air places. Very little has been done in this direction in England, but that little has justified the usefulness of the institution. In many of the large cities of the United States the demand for admission to these schools is so great that it cannot adequately be met by private enterprise. In New York Vacation schools have been adopted as part of the school system. " Holiday courses," consisting mostly of organised games, are also carried out in Berlin [1]

" Special Schools."

For purposes of these schools, defective children are classified into

(1) Mentally defective.
(2) Physically defective. These again are sub-divided according as they are
    (a) Physically defective other than blind and deaf.
    (b) Blind
    (c) Deaf

It will be convenient to deal with (1) and (2 a) first. Special regulations [2] have been issued by the Board of

[1] See Report of Mr. G. Andrew to the Scotch Education Department, 1904.

[2] See Circular May 13, 1904, concerning defective and epileptic children

Education concerning the school premises, terms of admission, and general treatment of these children No child is admitted under the age of seven or retained after reaching the age of sixteen

Most of the children of this type find their way into these special departments through the agency of the head teachers of the ordinary schools, whose duty it is to present defective children to the medical officer for examination on the occasions of his visits to the "special" department Every child, before admission, must be certified by the local authority's medical officer as defective

The hours during which a special school is open must not exceed two and a half in the morning and two in the afternoon; and the time table must provide for instruction in (1) reading, writing and arithmetic (elements), (2) singing and recitation, (3) object lessons, (4) drawing, (5) needlework for girls, (6) physical exercises, (7) manual instruction—a wide interpretation is given to this

The law demands, further, that the children be examined "from time to time" by the medical officer, and that proper records be kept The practice generally is for the medical officer to visit twice a year, and re-examine the scholars When any child, under thirteen years, has made sufficient advancement and is otherwise fit, he is drafted to one of the ordinary school departments

A sharp line is drawn between the physically and mentally defective in educational treatment. Separate buildings are therefore generally provided for them In the case of the merely physically defective children (cripples, etc.) whose education has been retarded through illness, it is generally found that they have normal capacity hence the curriculum for them is not so restricted. Specially constructed desks and chairs, and all those easy conveniences in the way of furniture and equipment which a benevolent foresight can supply, are often found associated with these centres   A trained nurse is usually attached to each centre, ambulances bring cripples and invalids from home to school and back again, and arrangements are commonly made through voluntary aid, the parents bearing part of the expense, to give these afflicted little ones some sustaining refreshment at midday

The Blind and Deaf.

By the Elementary Education (Blind and Deaf Children) Act 1893, it is incumbent on every educational authority to provide an "efficient and suitable" education for blind and deaf children resident in the district The same authority must also enforce the law of compulsory attendance, in the case of blind children from five to sixteen years of age, and in the case of the deaf from seven to sixteen years

Separate schools are provided for these, which may be either day or residential schools   Both kinds are found in some educational areas   The children receive instruction in the ordinary school subjects, particular attention being given to manual and industrial training, as deftness of hand and craft knowledge mostly form the only source of a livelihood when the school career is closed

As these schools cannot be built within reasonable distance of *every* child's home, travelling expenses, in *day* school cases, are allowed to children living beyond walking distance from the school; and guides sometimes are also provided for those who are too young to travel alone   The blind children are now usually taught reading and writing on the Braille system   The manual training includes work in mat-weaving, clay modelling, straw-plaiting, rug and basket making, chair-caning, typewriting, woodwork, bent-iron work, and the domestic arts for girls

In the case of the deaf the "oral" (or speech and lip-reading) system is generally adopted as the chief means of instruction Sometimes the "combined system" is used which includes the "oral" with manual signs The manual training course comprises cane and cardboard work, stencilling, tailoring, boot-making, woodwork, and the usual domestic subjects for girls

It is almost unnecessary to say that small classes in all these "special schools" are essential to efficiency It is not uncommon to find one teacher to fifteen or sixteen scholars, or even less In the woodwork classes ten is the limit for London County Council schools.

An "after care" committee to safeguard the interests of these defective children, and especially to secure them suitable employment, when they have attained the leaving age, has been found a useful institution

It is worthy of note that a unique experiment is being tried in Mannheim, where *intermediate* schools have been established—*intermediate*, that is, between the "special" and the ordinary school These have been founded because (1) it has been shown that ten per cent of the children in the elementary schools are unable to keep pace with the progress of the scholar with average ability; (2) it is considered that such children need special educational and hygienic treatment; (3) it is further considered that the presence of these children in the same class with others of higher mental capabilities and better physique tends to retard general progress This system of auxiliary classes is called the "Förkenklassen" system[1]

[1] See Report of the Medical Officer of the late School Board for London, 1904.

CHAPTER IV.

DISCIPLINE

DISCIPLINE is the essence of government It is the sum of the acts of a school directed to the training of the body and the cultivation of the mind It expresses itself in orderliness, in conduct, and in the ways and means by which the school as a whole is governed It concerns itself chiefly with child development, and especially with the formation of character. It should teach the child what to love and what to avoid and lay the foundation of self-inspection and self-control As conduct, in the words of Matthew Arnold, is "three-fourths of life," so it may be said that discipline, in its broadest sense, is the whole life of a school, the rest being merely accessories.

As the laws of a nation, combined with the public conscience, give the standard of public morality, so do the laws of a school, added to the influence of its chief, give the standard of school discipline If the discipline is sound, the school tone is certain to be sound also, for tone is both the voluntary and involuntary manifestations of the moral attributes of a school, the spirit of which is making its presence felt

Good tone therefore implies sound discipline, which from the class point of view has been already discussed, and the main principles in relation thereto indicated Those principles have a general application Some points, however, remain to be stated in connection with the school department.

There are, of course, certain fundamental principles
which the good disciplinarian always accepts for his guidance in whatever class or school he may be placed   There
are, however, auxiliary aids which have to be enlisted
according to the ages, attainments, and sex of the scholars;
and there arises also in relation to these the question as to
the degree of application which the fundamental principles
should receive

It is evident, for example, that the discipline which often
characterises a good boys' department would not be, as a
whole, equally suitable for a girls' school. Again, the
discipline that might be admirably adapted to a girls'
department would be altogether out of place in a school
for infants Similar differentiation is often necessary in
the treatment of children in the various classes of a department The kind of discipline that is suitable for infants
between three and four years of age is not equally applicable to children between six and seven Indeed it may be
said that as a child ascends through the three grades of an
infant school, the discipline should correspondingly rise in
its demands upon him

These remarks apply with almost equal force, but with
some variations, to the classes in the senior departments
The children of the lower classes must be made to feel the
irresistible power of external forces, whether they are natural
or conventional The iron hand, however, ought to be
covered with the velvet glove. But the upper classes, and
particularly the first class, do not, as a rule, need exactly
the same disciplinary treatment The scholars there have
already passed through the earlier stages of a firm disciplinary régime, and have, in all probability, been guided
thereby and shaped their habits accordingly. They are
drawing nigh to the threshold of the labour world, and
each must soon play his part without a mentor by his side

It is desirable therefore that the older pupils especially should learn to govern themselves collectively and individually whilst kindly corrective powers are at hand, of which, as far as possible, they should be unconscious. One of the symptoms of perfect discipline is the scholars' unconsciousness of the existence of law, for law ceases to exist when full obedience is rendered to it.

Of course, self-government should be inculcated in every stage of school life, but its indispensable nature must be insisted upon in application to the older scholars.

Before quitting the essentially spiritual side of this subject as distinguished from that which deals with mere routine, it is desirable to state what those fundamental principles are upon which every kind of good departmental discipline must rest. These must appeal successfully to the three sides of a child's nature. It may be laid down therefore

(1) *That the premises and routine of the school must be such as to ensure to each scholar reasonable bodily comfort.* Good ventilation, suitable desks, and change of work and position are therefore necessary.

(2) *That moral beauty should be loved and moral depravity condemned.* Opportunities of exciting pleasurable emotions by the contemplation of moral attributes or the sight of natural beauty ought therefore to be seized whenever possible. Of course, it is equally important that vicious qualities should excite emotions of pain. " Character is higher than intellect. A great soul will be strong to live, as well as to think."[1]

(3) *That the intellectual and imaginative faculties must be trained.* Imaginative power appears to wane after a child has passed its sixth year. This is probably

[1] Emerson.

because little or no pains are taken to cultivate this
power that helps to colour life as the sun colours
the flowers.   Napoleon used to say, " You can only
govern men by imagination · without imagination
they are brutes   'Tis by speaking to the soul you
electrify them "

(4) *That the law of the school must be based on natural
law, and a knowledge of child life*   It should give
rewards for obedience and punishment for neglect.

(5) *That while discipline is framed to meet the collective
attributes of children, it should be regulated as far as
possible to meet each child's natural disposition*   A
word of kind reproof will work wonders with one
pupil, while to another severe rebuke or even
stronger measures must be applied

(6) *That the teachers should be in sympathy with child
nature* and respect its natural tendencies and
reasonable desires   "Sympathy is our best friend
in education."[1]

" The entire object of true education is to make people
not merely do the right things, but enjoy the right things ;
not merely industrious, but to love industry, not merely
learned, but to love knowledge; not merely pure, but to
love purity, not merely just, but to hunger and thirst
after justice."[2]

Esprit de corps is the child of good discipline   It is the
beneficent spirit that animates the school as a whole   It
is the scholars' devotion to the school's fundamental laws,
to its interests, and to its honour.

Of all the many ramifications associated with school
organisation, few are more important than the work of
routine and enlisted aids that have for their object the

[1] Miss Edgeworth   [2] Ruskin.

formation of good habits and the general furtherance of
the high aim which discipline has in view   Brief notice of
these under various heads, is desirable.

Attendance

The value of punctual and regular attendance to a
school, a class and the individual scholar is undoubted
A high level of efficiency, uninterrupted progress in the
courses of instruction, and habits of systematic and
punctual attention to duty can only be secured when the
attendance is quite satisfactory

Although in educational administration the teacher is
not held directly responsible for regular attendance, yet it
may be generally said that when the sum of the school
influences is good, the regularity of the scholars fairly
corresponds with it   It is, moreover, always considered
creditable to a department when the percentage of attendance is high, notwithstanding the responsibility of the
bye-law officers in these matters   But the punctual side
of attendance is one, perhaps, that lies more immediately
within the range of the teacher's office   If there is any
weakness in this respect, it is generally found that the
regularity suffers also

The organiser therefore ought to leave no stone un-
turned in the endeavour to obtain that high degree of
punctuality which may lie within the possibilities of the
locality in which the school is situated   Punctual and
regular attendance ought to be coveted for its own sake,
apart from the immediate or ultimate advantages in the
way of school efficiency   It is, however, a mistake to raise it
almost to the position of a divinity   The "perfect week" is
an ideal institution, its perfection consisting in the punctual
attendance, each session, of every scholar on the roll during
a given week   In other words, the "perfect week" repre-

sents the percentage of attendance as 100 Such weeks in
a large school can only come by miracle, or by overstrain-
ing the motives for good attendance and giving them a
glamour which is not naturally their own It is conceiv-
able that children, acting under the zealous and magnetic
influence of a strong head teacher, may be led to attend
school under circumstances that make it desirable they
should remain at home, both in the interest of their own
health and that of the scholars with whom they are
brought into contact The " perfect week ' is excellent as
an aim provided the pupils are safeguarded by advisory
precautions It is, of course, easier to get a week's perfection of attendance in a small school than in a large one,
since the adverse possibilities are reduced

Rewards

The term *rewards* ranges in meaning from words of
commendation to valuable prizes of permanent form In
the United States prizes in the school sense are extremely
rare, whereas in this country their usefulness is recognised
in most, if not in all, schools

It is a fairly common practice to give cards and prizes
for punctual and regular attendance provided the conduct
is quite satisfactory ; but each school when under isolated
management, and each educational area, has had its own
system

Cards, however, are usually awarded for punctual and
regular attendance either weekly or quarterly or both
Prizes, mostly in the form of books, are awarded annually
on the basis of the year's attendances, a very small margin
of absences being generally allowed, to meet either exceptional or well-recognised demands It is best not to
give prizes in an infant school In some districts the
local authority, limiting and varying the amount per head

to be expended on each standard or class according as it is
the lowest or highest, has allowed the head teacher of each
department to draw up his or her own scheme for awarding
prizes, on the basis of attendance, conduct, and progress.
Such a scheme is in existence in London, and is, in its
main features, set out below :—

"Prizes are awarded to scholars attending the schools
partly as a stimulus to attendance and partly as a reward
for conduct and industry, according to a scheme to be
drawn up by the head teacher, with the approval of the
managers.

"A statement of the grounds on which the prizes are to
be allotted must be drawn up by the head teacher and
approved by the managers before the educational year
begins, and hung up, framed, in the hall or in a class-room,
so that all the children may know what they have to aim
at Such scheme should set forth (a) the grounds on
which prizes are to be given, and (b) the amount to be
allowed in prizes for each class or standard.

"An amount calculated at the following rates, reckoned
on the average attendance for the year ended on the last
Friday before Lady-day preceding the commencement of
the educational year is allowed annually for prizes, viz. :—

Scholars below Standard I		¾d.	per head
Scholars in Standard I		1d	do
Do	II.	2d	do
Do	III.	2½d	do
Do	IV	3½d	do
Do	V	4¾d	do.
Do	VI	6d	do
Do	VII	10½d	do
Scholars in special schools (includ-			
ing blind, deaf, physically and			
mentally deficient)		4d	do "

The principle on which medals are awarded is further indicated thus —

"A medal is awarded to every full-time scholar (with the exception of those children in infants' departments who at the close of the educational year are below Standard I.) who has attended punctually on every occasion on which the school has been open during the year ending July, and also to every half-time scholar who has attended punctually half the times the school has been open during the same year; provided that absence on not more than four half-days or two whole days in a year shall not debar any child from receiving a medal, if at least two days' written notice of such absence has been sent by the parent or guardian of the child.

"The first three medals awarded to a scholar will be of white metal, the fourth and fifth of bronze, and the sixth, seventh, eighth, ninth, and tenth of gilded bronze, and the eleventh of silver. Scholars gaining a tenth medal will also be presented with a framed engraving"[1]

Badges

Some head teachers, acting on their own initiative, have instituted badges to be worn by scholars whose exemplary conduct has been considered worthy of a distinguishing mark. The badge, however, does not become the personal property of the scholar, like the prizes and medals, but is liable to be taken away should there be any lapse from the standard of good behaviour which merited distinction.

Banners, Flags, School Ladder, etc.

It has been found a useful stimulus to the class, as distinguished from the individual pupil, to give into its weekly keeping a banner or flag for meritorious conduct

[1] See L.C.C. Education Code, 1904.

and the best attendance during any particular week   This
induces a friendly rivalry between class and class which
reacts on the individual scholar who is disposed to be
absent occasionally and unnecessarily from school   Another good plan, tending in the same beneficial direction, is
represented by the "school ladder," which, hung in a conspicuous position, indicates, during any one week, the
relative positions of merit, in regard to attendance, of each
class in the school.

Again, the *Friday half-hour* has proved of value as an
incentive to excellent class attendance, the last half-hour
of the final session of the week being devoted to play in the
case of the class or classes that have reached a certain high
percentage of attendance   The privilege of being dismissed
before their other schoolfellows apparently has its charms
Care must be taken, in connection with this practice, that
the necessary two hours secular instruction is given in
senior departments   It may become necessary on this
account to reduce the half-hour to 20 minutes ; but even
then experience shows that the charm remains unbroken.

Ethics of Rewards.

Is it advisable to give rewards or prizes for good attendance at school?   Although *conduct* and *progress* are generally combined with attendance for this purpose the
rewards in practice really rest almost exclusively on
attendance, for that presupposes to a large extent the
other two   The motive for such prizes does not reach the
great majority of the scholars, and probably nearly all
those who secure prizes would attend just as well without
having the prospect of rewards in view.   But the worst
feature of the case is that attendance prizes weaken rather
than strengthen the obligation to be regular at school,
which each child ought to be made to feel as keenly as

possible. They probably tend, too, to foster a desire for material gain rather than a sense of duty Obviously, good attendance has its own rewards Good attendance generally implies progress ; and every child delights in the power conferred by added physical or mental strength

If, however, prizes are awarded in a school, they ought to be few in number and relatively difficult of attainment, sustained effort being indispensable In some schools prizes are given for (1) good conduct and (2) proportionate success in studies Sometimes each class is annually allowed, with proper safeguards, to select by ballot one or more of its members who have distinguished themselves by good character throughout the year *Proportionate* success does not necessarily enable the cleverest children to carry off the prizes, but renders it possible for the dullest scholar, by supreme effort, to master difficulties, to receive due recognition in this respect, the teacher of course being the sole judge The test in this case would naturally be the sum total of the records for a term or year, and not a final examination,—making proper adjustments for age, application, and degree of ability

The true value of a prize is measured by the extent and intensity of the effort to secure it It is the honour associated with the possession of a prize and not its monetary value that constitutes the real motive for great and prolonged exertion This motive power could be made to have a wider application if prizes were always awarded on a truly equitable basis, instead of allowing natural talent to get all, or nearly all, the spoils of victory

It is thought that certificates artistically designed, suitably worded, and worthy of permanent preservation, would serve all the laudable purposes which now underlie the award of prizes Certificates, of course, would have to be graded, those of the highest type being few and very difficult of attainment They might be classified into (1) certificates of honour, (2) certificates of merit, and (3) certificates of proficiency.

The timely and judicious use of praise in the ordinary course of school work will, however, often effect more good than the remoter prizes and certificates Scholarships are awards of rather a different type to those which have been considered. No one will be disposed to find fault with the principle of giving clever and industrious children an opportunity of obtaining the fullest educational benefits that the country's institutions afford.

Punishments

The true art of discipline lies in the complete government of children without their consciousness of restraint. The controlling power of the teacher falls away, therefore, from this ideal in so far as resort to punishment becomes necessary Hence every task imposed, every censure administered, and every measure of restraint applied implies some defect in the machinery of government,—each is a confession of failure to influence a pupil by the best and most lasting means All punishment is in itself an evil.

The necessity, however, for some form of restraint or chastisement to meet exceptional cases is wisely and generally recognised Punishment is the lesser evil applied to avoid the greater one that lives in the future A closer study of the individual characters of children would often obviate the necessity for punishment. The ordinary child is charged with activities, and it is his delight to give expression to them Good discipline should keep those activities adequately and educationally employed Variations in disposition account for the different potentialities shown by children and their tendency to run in certain directions

It is these variations, in connection with large classes, that make a teacher's work so difficult. Under such circumstances it becomes a practical impossibility to adequately and always allow for the personal equation in directing the activities in question, and therefore unless the self-control of the child is great, or implicit obedience has become a habit, there must necessarily be some individual breach of order or instructions. Such breach is a child's safety-valve for the time being. The child, however, must be made, for its own sake, to render obedience, to cultivate will power, and thus keep its activities under proper control.

Forms of Punishment

Punishments usually assume the form of (1) caution or censure, (2) deprivations, (3) impositions, (4) corporal punishment, and (5) expulsion.

Censure

It has been already implied, if not directly stated, that punishment ought to be used sparingly. Continual fault-finding does harm. Bonâ-fide attempts to eradicate a bad habit or to overcome a difficulty are materially aided by a kind word at every successful or half-successful step, while upbraidings for clumsiness or lack of wit, etc., have quite the opposite tendency. Some inexperienced teachers are prone, on the commission of an offence or blunder, to hurl a battalion of unkind words at the scholar, recalling past offences and faults. Such action is mischievous. On the other hand, the love of approbation in children is strong. It ought therefore to be taken advantage of on every proper occasion.

Reproach for past offences is poison in a child's veins, whereas apt praise will sometimes raise a giant beanstalk in a night. The Bourbons "learnt nothing and *forgot*

nothing." The world knows their fate; and failure can
be foreshadowed for every one who does likewise, in all
walks of life.

Private censure is, as a rule, best. If, however, the
offence is a moral one, committed openly in class, then it
is probably best to denounce the offence, and censure the
offender, openly also. But whatever is done, observance
of the principle applicable to all punishment is desirable,
viz., the censure should not go beyond the minimum point
necessary to secure the object in view. Excess kills the
purpose of censure, and weak denunciation minimises the
nature of the offence in the minds of the children.

Deprivations.

Deprivations include (1) loss of marks, (2) loss of place.
It is assumed that every school has its system of good conduct marks. It is needless to say that misbehaviour ought
not, under any circumstances, to affect the marks given in
the ordinary subjects of instruction. Assuming that right
influences are at work at home, and that the parents are
periodically communicated with as to a child's progress,
the loss of marks for indifferent conduct ought to be an
effective weapon.

Loss of place may follow from loss of marks for poor
conduct. Loss of place may assume several forms, e.g.,
(1) temporary disgrace—as when a scholar is removed from
his usual place in class for some minor but persistent fault
—such removal not lasting for longer than one or two
sessions. (2) Loss of play at the recreation interval.
(3) Deprivation of the right to play for the school in a
sports match. (4) Detention after school hours. (5) Loss
of certificate or prize wholly or partially dependent on
good conduct. Of these (2) is the least satisfactory. This
should never be put into operation against a class as a

whole, for reasons too obvious to mention, quite apart from the demands of ventilation

Detention after school hours ought not to be allowed to exceed half-an-hour, with or without impositions. It is usual to have a rota of teachers for this purpose, as without close supervision detention is next to useless. This is a fairly good remedy for careless work or persistent inattention Any imposition insisted upon during this time ought as far as possible to have reference to the loss occasioned by carelessness or inattention Generally speaking, however, enforced inactivity is a great punishment

Impositions.

It is well to avoid the meaningless pernicious drudgery that consists in writing a word or phrase a hundred or more times, and also the task of committing to memory some portion of the Bible It is not good to associate the Bible with restraint and compulsion If *writing* is imposed, it is best to associate it with an element of interest or profit, and not lifeless routine, so that the maximum good may result.

Corporal Punishment and its Ethics.

Corporal punishment, next to expulsion, should be the *dernier ressort* It is generally considered more efficacious if administered in private, and after the lapse of an hour or thereabouts from the time the offence was committed. Circumstances, however, may arise when it may be deemed desirable to administer such punishment before the whole school It is manifestly improper for a teacher to inflict corporal punishment when harbouring feelings of resentment against the offender. Much of the value of punishment is also lost if administered while the offender is not

in a normal condition of mind, that is, in a state of anger
or excitement   Of course, every offender ought to have a
reasonable opportunity of defence.

In some American schools trial by jury for moral
delinquency has been introduced, the teacher acting as
judge. The Principal of Thayer Street School, Providence,
says:[1] " I have made each schoolroom a separate unit of
organisation, on the basis of continual self-government,
with reference not only to the larger matters, but to all the
details of discipline. The pupils in each room choose each
month, by ballot, a committee on self-government, consisting of five members.   It is the special duty of this
committee to take notice of any offences against good order
and propriety.

" At some proper time, usually at the close of the school,
the chairman of the committee presides over the class and
presents the charges against offenders   The pupil charged
is allowed to say what he chooses in defence or explanation,
and the pupils decide by vote what the punishment shall
be. The teacher is an *ex-officio* member of the committee,
and places in the hands of the committee any complaints
which she may have to make against any pupils   She
reserves a power of veto which she exercises in case the
judgment of the pupils at any time seems to be improper."

This plan the principal states has been attended with
the happiest results. " The attitude of the school, as a
whole, exhibits a marked change   In most of the rooms
the notion that the teacher is to watch the children to
prevent disorder and idleness has passed away   There is
quite as good order when the teacher is absent from the
room as when she is present   This plan has seemed to be
especially successful in developing a feeling of *social responsibility*"

[1] Volume 10, p 135, Special Reports

This Theyer Street scheme of government is a modification of the "school city" plan as carried out in some New York schools. The "school city" plan aims at governing a school by means of its pupils in a similar way to that adopted by citizens in the government of a city.

In all schools in which corporal punishment is regarded as necessary — and it is so regarded in most schools, the United States and France being conspicuous exceptions — care should be taken to see that the same standard is maintained throughout the school, that the offender should understand that the punishment is a regrettable necessity, and that mercy is always allowed to season justice.

Herbert Spencer advocates corporal punishment. As want of obedience to natural law inevitably brings punishment, so a breach of rules framed for a child's benefit ought to bring pain and penalties—they are a foretaste of the reality of things in adult life when laws are violated.

On the other hand, it is claimed by the opponents of corporal punishment that it represents *brute force enthroned*, and that in its absence the teacher has the wholesome discipline of both governing himself and keeping the scholars always fully interested and suitably employed. They think the teacher should learn " to walk without a stick."

Certainly much harm may be done if corporal punishment is not inflicted with discrimination. It should, of course, never be used for delicate and emotional children.

Bell thought that deprivation was the best kind of punishment, while Lancaster pinned his faith to ridicule.

In many educational areas rules have been formulated by the local authority for the guidance of teachers. In London, for example, corporal punishment may only be administered for "grave moral offences," and not even then till "other methods have been tried and failed."

The head teacher, too, is held responsible for all punishments of whatever kind; but he may delegate the power
to inflict "slight punishment" to those assistants whom
he may consider worthy of the trust

As the teacher ought to be an exemplary citizen and not
break the law, it is well to briefly notice the legal aspect
of this question

By the common law of England, any kind of what is
known as unlawful restraint or punishment applied to a
child by a teacher is actionable, and renders the teacher
liable to fine or imprisonment. Justification can, however, be successfully pleaded when, in the words of Lord
Chief Justice Cockburn, the punishment is "moderate and
reasonable." Judgment in the following cases briefly
summarises the law on this point

In *Regina* v. *Hopley* the Lord Chief Justice Cockburn,
in giving judgment, said —

"By the law of England, the parent or the schoolmaster, who for
this purpose represents the parent, and has the parental authority
delegated to him, may, for the purpose of correcting what is evil in
the child, inflict moderate and reasonable corporal punishment, always
however with this condition, that it is moderate and reasonable. If it
be administered for the gratification of passion or rage, or if it be pro-
tracted beyond the child's power of endurance, or with an instrument
unfitted for the purpose and calculated to produce danger to life or
limb, in all such cases the punishment is excessive and violent, and is
unlawful."

In *Gardner* v *Bygrave* Mr Justice Mathew said, in
giving judgment. —

"The point for the court was whether, according to the law of
England, it was criminal for a master to cane a pupil by striking him
on the hand. The magistrate stated that the boy deserved the punishment, and he did not attack the right to punish corporally with the
view to intellectual stimulation, as the counsel for the respondent had
done. It was clear that no injury was caused in that case, and the
punishment was properly inflicted. The reason given by the magis-

trate, 'that caning on the hand, however inflicted, was necessarily attended by serious injury,' was not sufficient to justify this conviction. It must, therefore, be quashed."

It was held, too, in *Cleary* v *Booth*—

"That besides the reasonable authority of a parent or guardian which is delegated to the schoolmaster, the schoolmaster had also the power to inflict corporal punishment upon a pupil for misconduct on the way to and from the school, and out of school hours"

Expulsion.

Expulsion is fraught with such serious consequences that it should only be resorted to when the school's resources have been taxed to the utmost and have failed, and when the continued presence of the offender in the school is likely to be a serious menace to its discipline It is well for the teacher not to accept sole responsibility for expulsion, but to enlist the aid and authority of the managers The Board of Education has taken up a definite position on this question and will support the managers' action if "reasonable ground" can be adduced for exclusion

The Punishment Book.

The punishment book is a necessary adjunct to corporal punishment [1] This book should contain the following items in connection with each case—date, name of scholar, offence, instrument of punishment, mode and amount of punishment, and signature of the teacher responsible.

Parents' and Managerial Aid.

It is hardly possible to over-estimate the value of a strong sympathetic link between the home and the school The

[1] See Schedule IV., Code 1901.

home sentiment is one of the most sacred things in life—it
may be said to stand next to that of religion The wise
teacher usually finds the means of ingratiating himself
into the hearts of the parents, well knowing that even a
small place there will help him in the work of training
Visits to the parents are strongly recommended whenever
practicable The parents, too, ought to be encouraged to
visit the teacher at school when any doubt arises in their
minds as to the treatment their children are receiving or
the progress they are making. Courteous and considerate
attention to complaints and requests, even when not made
in the best possible manner, is the wisest course always.
One disaffected parent, with a reasonable ground of com-
plaint, can do much mischief. The school and homes are
units in an association having a common interest and, to a
great extent, a common aim The unexpressed desire
characterises both,—that the children might learn to "do
justly, love mercy, and walk humbly" through life.

In many schools the influence for good which the Committee of Managers would be glad to exercise is not
adequately utilised Without suggesting anything in the
form of interference with the internal management of the
school, it is submitted that the managers willingness and
ability to help might be usefully directed The teacher
cannot afford to disregard any local force that will aid him
in the consummation of his work. Cases of difficulty with
parents, as well as with children, might well invoke the
individual or collective help of the managers A visit to
the house or a letter from the chairman has often been
found the turning point in a new and worthy career for a
child, or a fresh and agreeable departure from old ways on
the part of the parent The managers have proved
especially helpful in some poor districts by adopting a
system of home visitation as school circumstances invited.

This is usually done by the ladies All school functions such as annual excursions, prize distributions, open sessions, boot clubs, juvenile friendly societies, and organisations for underfed children, are favourable opportunities for the managers to be brought into contact with parents and children

Other Aids to Discipline.

Other aids to discipline are (1) annual excursions, (2) reports to parents, (3) annual prize distribution meeting, (4) open sessions, (5) savings bank, (6) home lessons, (7) the school library, (8) leagues of purity, of mercy, of courtesy, (9) school clubs, (10) underfed children organisation, (11) school lists, (12) office routine, (13) the hall address, (14) the honour and merit award, (15) the school motto, (16) the school cap and badge, (17) public examinations, (18) the school journey, (19) fire drill, (20) May Queen festival for girls, (21) Fairy Queen and Maypole fête for infants, (22) the old scholars' club, and (23) the school journal.

Some of these helps call for brief explanation or expansion All teachers are acquainted with the pleasurable anticipation that belongs to a child months before the annual Sunday School treat takes place, and the almost delirium of joy that is his when the happy day has arrived. A similar annual outing is a desirable institution for every day school; indeed, the practice in this direction is growing. All agencies for good become the more effective by being closely associated with happy hours in the lives of children Association between parents and teachers on occasions like these strengthens the link that cannot afterwards be easily strained or broken.

Reports to Parents

Periodical reports to parents are desirable As a child has a natural wish to please its parents, it is the more likely, knowing these reports to be inevitable, to put forth consistent effort at school and to endeavour to secure the approbation of the teacher by good conduct It is best to avoid long intervals between reports of this kind Quarterly or term reports are considered the most useful. The points to accentuate in these communications are conduct, progress in the various subjects, and attendance The form given below is a suitable one

REPORT TO PARENTS.[1]

SCHOLARS' ATTENDANCE, CONDUCT AND PROGRESS

For the   ended   190

Name   Standard

No of Scholars in Class   Place in Class

Number of Times the School was open

Times absent   Times late

	1	2		1	2	Additional Subjects :	1	2
Scripture			English					
Reading			History					
Writing			Geography					
Arithmetic			Needlework					
Spelling			Home Work					
Drawing			Conduct					

—   —   Head Teacher.

——————————— Class Teacher.

Columns 1   Maximum number of marks obtainable
   „   2   Marks obtained in each subject.
[1] The Report Form should be headed by the name of the School

Open Sessions.

Open sessions, once a year, have been found useful During these sessions,—two, as a rule, are ample—the ordinary school work proceeds as usual, and the parents are invited to visit the school and see its working arrangements It is a general practice on these occasions to exhibit some of the work that has been done during the preceding twelve months. The open session is one of pleasure to the parents and of delight to the children

Home Lessons.

Home lessons, given with discrimination, are valuable adjuncts to school work. They represent more than anything else the projection of the school into the home They help to show parents the reality of the progress their children are making; they become, under proper limitations, a unifying power in the association to which reference has already been made. Home lessons further render material assistance in the direction of private effort, without which self-reliance is an impossibility

It is well to remember that, under normal conditions, a reasonable day's work for a child has been done at the close of the afternoon session In order to prevent overstrain, therefore, the home lessons ought to be able to be mastered in time varying from thirty minutes to an hour, according to the age and attainments of the scholar. The work given ought always to be within the circle of the year's course of instruction and should refer generally to the application of what has been already taught What is demanded should, of course, be reasonably within the range of the average child's powers, and be of such a nature generally as to compel the scholar to rely entirely upon himself for its just accomplishment. Home lessons

that lend themselves to external and are often mischievous
in their effects   Home lessons ought to be regarded as
home duties.   In this spirit a high standard of accuracy
and neatness should be demanded, and the work thoroughly
and regularly tested.   It is manifest that home lessons are
out of place for infants

Two of the Mosely Commissioners say in regard to home
lessons in the United States—"Each child takes care of
his own sets of books, carries them home and uses them
there.   Indeed home lessons seem to be general except
among the very young children"[1]

Again, "The amount of home work done is more than
we could obtain in England   Parents in America like to
see what the children are doing in school, and make
proper arrangements for the child to study at home"[2] .

Underfed Children.

Underfed children, ill clad and ill shod as well, are not
uncommon in many urban schools.   Sickly complexions,
pinched faces, emaciated limbs and other outward signs of
the need of regular and proper nourishment are often too
apparent   A hungry child is necessarily unfit to receive
all the benefits to be derived from attendance at school
The seeds of organic disease are frequently sown through
continued ill-nourishment

In the absence of voluntary organisations to meet cases
like these, it is the teacher's duty to seek assistance elsewhere   The well-to-do children, in some schools, bring
boots and other articles of clothing to aid their less fortu-
nate school-fellows—do it, that is, unobtrusively through the
head teacher; but the feeding difficulty must be met by

[1] Mr. H. Coward, Mosely Education Commission Report, 1904

[2] Rev. A. W. Jephson, Mosely Education Commission Report,
1904.

other means. No child receiving help in clothing or food
ought to feel degraded. The food should be the manna in
the wilderness. It is scarcely necessary to remind the
teacher that "kind hearts are more than coronets," that
"mercy is twice blessed," and that in the absence of the
true spirit of charity all are as "sounding brass or a
tinkling cymbal."

The School Library

This ought to be considered indispensable. Its value in
forming character, in encouraging application, in reaching
the home, and in many other ways, is undoubted. In the
United States every school appears either to possess a good
library of its own or to be directly associated with the
public library, which co-operates with the school for the
purpose of supplying it with suitable books. The following extracts from Mr. H. R. Rathbone's report (Mosely
Commission) will be found interesting: "A separate
department for children has existed in the Boston Public
Library since 1895. It occupies two rooms, one for
recreative reading and the other for study, both furnished
with low tables, chairs, and book-cases. Children over the
age of ten years can be card holders and may draw two
books at a time. In the reference room (study room)
lessons are studied, compositions written, and other pre-
parations for school are done. One feature of the room
which is constantly proving its value is the collection of
text-books used in the Boston Public Schools. Teachers
are invited to come to the Library with classes and themselves to give instruction or make use of books reserved
for them as they may request. Books are sent to the
schools by the branch department which has a special
collection for deposit. Complete freedom is allowed
teachers to make their own choice of books, no record of

circulation is required, and the books may be kept weeks or months as desired." Mr. Rathbone further says that advice and assistance in the selection of books are given to the children by the officials in charge of the children's department.

Leagues of Purity, of Mercy, Guild of Courtesy

Leagues and guilds of this character are usually associated with wide organisations external to the school, to which scholars may belong, a badge or miniature medal being worn by the children to indicate membership. In order to become a member a child has to make a promise to adhere to the principles on which the league or guild is founded. It is important that due care be exercised before admission to membership is allowed, which ought to be regarded as a privilege only to be obtained by a probationary period of good conduct on the lines upon which the league or guild is founded. Solemn promises made and soon broken do more harm than good.

School Lists.

School lists giving the names of pupils who have distinguished themselves by exemplary conduct, punctual and regular attendance, close industry, or general progress, act as a stimulus to some who are not readily responsive to ordinary school influences. They also serve to maintain a standard of high aim when that has been once reached.

Office Routine

It is usual in most good schools to have posts of honour for highly deserving pupils who perform monitorial duties of various kinds, certain other privileges being generally attached to office. The circle of influence is widened by not confining these posts to a selected few, but by conferring them on all scholars in rotation who show they are worthy of trust and confidence. Such rotation, too, reduces the possibility of annoyance which sometimes comes from those who consider themselves permanent tenants-at-will The election by ballot, once a month or once a term, of a class captain by the pupils, who is responsible, next to the teacher, for the proper conduct of the class, has been found a useful step in the direction of pupil self-government. But nowhere has this principle of self-government been carried out so successfully as in America.

The Hall Address

Both in Germany and America the hall address is much practised. In the latter country it is sometimes given daily in a very brief way, usually preceded by reading some portion of the Scriptures without comment

Once a week, if the school building lends itself to such an assembly, it is desirable for the head teacher to give an address to the whole school, the chief aim of which should be moral training It is hardly necessary to say that cold didactic lectures are quite useless for this purpose If any good is to result from these weekly addresses, the incidents upon which they turn should be drawn from realities—from contemporaneous events, from history, from the Bible—using these as the vehicle for the praise of virtue and the condemnation of vice Unless pleasurable emotions are excited in the contemplation of right-doing, and painful or contemptuous emotions by the review of wrong, ethical training cannot be directly effected

The Honour and Merit Board

This usually consists of a framed board on which are recorded the names of pupils who have obtained scholar-

ships or passed other examinations worthy of mention
Any noble acts performed by individual scholars ought to
find permanent expression on the school walls in a similar
way   These records especially serve to impress upon the
pupils the corporate life of the school and to give it a
historical interest

The School Journey.

The school journey is based on the idea of a country
holiday for the scholars, under the control and management of the teachers, as a combined source of health,
pleasure and education.

As the journey may vary considerably in length of time
and specific purpose, according to local circumstances, it is
probably best here to relate particulars of the journey as
carried out in a London school rather than give a descrip-
tion by mere generalisations.

In this school the Easter holiday is utilised for the
journey   The head teacher many weeks beforehand sends
a communication to the parents announcing the objective
of the journey and giving the probable cost, which has
varied during the past eight years from 21s to 23s 6d for
eight days

School journeys have been made to Abergavenny, Chep-
stow, Malvern, etc., these places being chiefly used as a
base for daily excursions   Generally about forty or fifty
scholars, from Standard III upwards, accompanied by
three or more teachers, form the party

Each boy is supplied with a hectographed guide-book of
about forty pages, which gives the following information :—

(1) The personal necessities for the outing, accompanied
with general instructions. (2) The time tables of the
outward and homeward journeys from London (3)
Incidents of these journeys—things to be seen and

observed on the way—*e.g.*, natural phenomena, centres of industry, public buildings, lines that meet at railway junctions, etc. (4) Itinerary for each day with brief notes on objects of interest. (5) Topographical maps, elevations and sections of hill ranges, geological sections of the various districts to be visited, sketches of fossils, etc. (6) Geological notes. (7) A list of the party. (8) Individual cash account, giving spaces for receipts and expenditure each day—checked daily by the teachers. (9) A blank register for the record of marks on conduct, cleanliness, and local knowledge. (10) An Index.

Al fresco and other lectures are given by the teachers. It is found that gentlemen of local standing gladly give their help to the party on matters in which they possess special knowledge, *e.g.*, a vicar shows the party over his church, or a dean over a cathedral, pointing out architectural characteristics and beauties, and colouring its existence with historical fact; a local scientist gives lectures *en marchant* on the geology of the district; or a retired colonel accompanies the party to an old battlefield, and fights the battle o'er again, or explains the mysteries of a fort or Roman camp.

To illustrate some of the things accomplished by the party on these journeys, the following will suffice: (1) Traced a tributary from its source to entry into the main stream. (2) Climbed hills over 1000 feet high, and noted the counties seen, elevations and depressions, towns and villages, great landmarks, etc. (3) Searched for fossils, each boy bringing home a small collection. (4) Visited places of historical interest, such as ancient camps, Roman and British.

Each lad is examined daily on the knowledge obtained from his previous day's work, and entries are made in his guide-book accordingly.

As to cost, (1) the Railway Company carries the children
at quarter fare   (2) Modest temperance hotels take the
children for 10s. or 11s. per week, including board, lodging,
and service

Many of the boys, as well as the teachers, carry a
camera   At the close of each journey a descriptive photo-
album is made, containing cuttings from the local press
and other descriptive matter, which is preserved as a
souvenir.

Some results   (1) Cordial relations between teachers,
scholars and parents   (2) The scholars' exceptional interest
in geography, geology, topography, and local history.   (3)
Strong tendency to improve the discipline and tone of the
school.

The School Motto

Each school ought to have its own motto, which should be
so simple as to appeal to every one of its scholars.   A motto
helps to give to a school a well-defined individuality, and
adds to its life another trait that distinguishes that school
from all others.   It crystallises the central point on which
the school's moral teaching hangs, and acts like a strong
cement in binding its units together.   History teaches how
a phrase giving clear definition to a great principle will
hold a multitude of people together, and transform them
in aim into a homogeneous whole   In selecting a school
motto it is well to request the parents, through the scholars,
to suggest a briefly expressed sentiment for the purpose
This is practicable in most districts   The head teacher
and staff could then select a few of those suggestions considered to be the best, and submit them to the vote of the
whole school, with the view of adopting the one motto
which most completely accords with the views of the

majority "The school should be the symbol of an eternal unifying spirit."[1]

Fire drill.

Fire drill is essential for every school. The schools must, at various times, be called upon suddenly and unexpectedly to go through this drill at a given signal. This signal is generally the ringing of hand or electric bells, and the object is, of course, to effect a speedy clearance of the building without undue haste or excitement Apart from the value of the drill as a safety measure in case of fire, it also trains the child to face unexpected and even dangerous situations with composure It is an object lesson too in the desirability of prompt obedience.

The May Queen Festival.

Once a year, in some girls' departments, the scholars are called upon to select their May Queen Simplicity and purity of character, combined with sweetness of disposition, invariably carry off the palm on these occasions. At the festival which follows the queen is enthroned and crowned, and the children show their deference to her quality and submission to her authority The Fairy Queen Fête is a similar institution for infant schools, the upper classes only taking part in the selection of the favoured one.

Clubs.

With regard to old scholars' clubs, it is lamentable to find, in large urban centres, scholars stepping over the threshold of the school at the leaving age, and never crossing it again They pass out of sight, like the shadow figures on the bridge in the vision of Mirzah.

[1] Words of the U.S. Commissioner of Education

The School Journal

The school journal, issued monthly, in printed form, is, as a rule, only practicable in large schools, assuming that it must pay its own expenses. A journal has, however, been found possible in small schools when taking hekto-graphed or typewritten form. It is so useful in a multi-tude of ways, especially in conveying both necessary and desirable information to parents and scholars, that the wonder is it has not been generally adopted. As a stimulus to thought among the scholars, whose compositions when of exceptional merit should be inserted in the journal, it has few rivals. But what is equally important is this—it is the monthly message from school to home.

In districts in which the schools do not lie very far apart it seems quite practicable and desirable to have a room, occupying a central position, fitted as a miniature printing office, for the use of the neighbouring schools. The upper standard scholars could then have one lesson a week in type-setting and printing—valuable instruction in itself—and thus be able to set up and print the journal for their own schools.

General Remarks

But these devices as aids to discipline will be next to useless unless thoroughness characterises all that are called into use. They are not intended to curb personal liberty, nor to restrain activities, but to guide and direct them to useful ends. "All things are moral. That soul which within us is a sentiment, outside of us is law." [1]

The admirable words contained in the Introduction to the Code of 1904 give an immutable standard of aim in all that concerns the discipline of a school. "Teachers can do

[1] Emerson

much to lay the foundations of conduct. They can endeavour, by example and influence, aided by the sense of discipline which should pervade the school, to implant in the children habits of industry, self-control, and courageous perseverance in the face of difficulties; they can teach them to reverence what is noble, to be ready for self-sacrifice, and to strive their utmost after purity and truth; they can foster a strong respect for duty, and that consideration and respect for others which must be the foundation of unselfishness and the true basis of all good manners; while the corporate life of the school, especially in the playground, should develop that instinct for fair-play and for loyalty to one another which is the germ of a wider sense of honour in later life.

"In all these endeavours the school should enlist, as far as possible, the interest and co-operation of the parents and the home in an united effort to enable the children not merely to reach their full development as individuals, but also to become upright and useful members of the community in which they live, and worthy sons and daughters of the country to which they belong."

CHAPTER V.

SCHOOL RECORDS AND REGISTRATION.

Both records and registration, on the lines laid down by the Board of Education, are necessary to obtain recognition as a public elementary school The principal objects of these are to have an historical account of the growth and development of the school as a whole or any variations in its numbers, its efficiency, or its staff, to have a statement concerning each scholar—his name, address, date of birth, progress, daily attendance and date of withdrawal, to supply the necessary figures and information to the Board of Education as a basis for the annual grant ; to supply information to the bye-law authority in order that attendance may be enforced, or exemption granted, and, finally, to have a properly authenticated record of reports received and grants allowed.

Every school must have three kinds of registers, viz, (1) the register of admission, progress and withdrawal, (2) the class attendance registers,[1] and (3) the summary register. The first and second of these are chiefly concerned with individual scholars while the last deals collectively with the groups of children in the form of classes, and with the school as a whole

[1] Including a half-time register if necessary.

164

The *general* conditions to be observed in regard to registration are thus laid down by the Board of Education[1]:—

"'Attendance' for the purpose of ascertaining the average attendance of a school, other than a higher elementary school, shall be reckoned exclusively in accordance with the following regulations

"(*a*) No attendance may be reckoned for any scholar under three or over fifteen years of age, or for any scholar while habitually employed as a monitor

"(*b*) For each infant present at secular instruction during one school meeting for a period of not less than one hour and a half there will be reckoned one attendance.

"(*c*) For each scholar other than an infant scholar present at secular instruction during one school meeting for a period of not less than two hours there will be reckoned one attendance ; and

"(*d*) for each such scholar who is a half-time scholar there will be reckoned, in addition, half an attendance, subject to the following limitation —

"the total of the additional attendances allowed in the case of any half-time scholar shall not exceed such a number as will, when added to the number of his two-hour attendances during the school year or portion of the year which has elapsed since he became a half-time scholar, exceed three-fourths of the number of the school openings in the corresponding period

"In making up the minimum time constituting an attendance there may be reckoned—

"(i) any time occupied by instruction, according to the approved time table, given to the scholars elsewhere than

[1] Arts. 43-49 and Schedule IV , Code 1904

at the school, in one of the *subjects named in Article* 4,[1] in drawing, in science, in physical exercises, or in any other subject specially recognised by the Board for the purpose of this Article

" (ii) any time occupied by visits paid during the school hours, with the sanction of the inspector, and under arrangements approved by him, to places of educational value or interest, provided that the whole time spent at such place or places be not less than one hour and a half; but not more than twenty attendances made up of such visits shall be reckoned for any one scholar in the same school year

" (iii) any time occupied by a central examination (other than for labour certificates) attended by scholars with the sanction of the inspector, provided that the time allowed for examination be not less than one hour and a half,

" (iv) any time occupied in attending at a training college or centre for pupil teachers for the purpose of model or criticism lessons

" The minimum time constituting an attendance must include an interval of ten minutes for recreation, and, if the meeting be of three, or, in the case of infants, of two and a half hours' duration, the interval may be fifteen minutes

" The school or department must have met not less than 400 times in the school year [2]

" Notice must be sent to the inspector as soon as is possible in each case, of every date upon which the school will be closed or its ordinary work suspended, whether for the holidays or for any special occasion, and in the event

[1] These subjects are handicraft, gardening, cookery (in seaport towns) for boys, cookery, laundry, dairy-work, household management for girls

[2] To this rule there are three exceptions   See Art 45, Code 1901

of failure to give timely notice a deduction of £1 will be made from the annual grant unless the managers or the local authority acted without timely notice by reason of a sudden emergency. Unless it is possible to give at least seven days' clear notice of an intended closure, such notice should be given by telegram.

" If the sanitary authority of the district in which the school is situated, or any two members thereof, acting on the advice of the Medical Officer of Health, require either the closure of the school or the exclusion of certain children for a specified time, with a view to preventing the spread of disease or any danger to health likely to arise from the condition of the school, such requirement must at once be complied with, but after compliance appeal may be made to the Board if the requirement is considered unreasonable."

The admission and daily attendance of the scholars must be carefully registered by, or under the supervision of the head teacher, and must be duly verified from time to time by the managers.

General Rules for the use of Registers

1. "The names of the school, of the department, and, in the case of attendance registers, of the class, must be distinctly written on the cover of each register, and on the title-page there must be the signature of the correspondent and the date on which it was issued to the teacher.

2. The pages of all registers must be numbered consecutively, no leaf must be inserted in or withdrawn from any register, and no blank spaces should be left between the entries.

3. Entries must be original and not copies, and must be made in ink without erasure or insertion.

" If it is necessary to make any correction this should be done in such a manner that the original entry and the alteration made are both clear on the face of the record.

4 Registers should be kept for ten years after they have been filled

The head teacher of a school or department is held responsible for the proper keeping and preservation of the records of that school or department, and should not delegate to a subordinate any part of this work except the keeping of attendance registers.

Pupil teachers of the first year may not be employed in registration, other pupil teachers may register the attendances of their own classes."

Special Rules for Admission Register

1 "An entry should be made in the admission register for each scholar on his admission to the school No name should be removed until the child is exempt from the legal obligation to attend school, unless it has been ascertained that he or she is dead, is attending another school, or has left the neighbourhood If no information is obtainable the name may be removed after a continuous absence of four weeks.

2 Successive numbers must be allotted to the scholars on their admission so that each may have his own number, which he should retain throughout his career in the school The number will then serve to identify him

When any scholar whose name has been removed from the register is readmitted a new entry must be made, but the scholar should resume his old number and cross reference should be made to the entries.

3 "This register must show distinctly for each scholar who has actually been present in the school—

(a) His number on the register

(b) The date of his admission (and re-admission)—day, month, and year

(c) His name *in full*

(d) The name and address of his parent or guardian

(e) Whether exemption from religious instruction is claimed on his behalf

(f) The exact date—day, month, and year of his birth

(g) The last school he attended before entering this school. If this is his first school, the word 'none' should be entered in this column

(h) If he has left, the date of his last attendance at *this* school and the cause of his leaving

4. This register should have an alphabetical index."

Rules as to the Provision of Attendance Registers.

1 "In each school or department in which both infants and other scholars are taught there must be separate sets of attendance registers kept for each, and no attendances may be transferred from one to the other

2 For each class in a school or department there should be a separate attendance register, containing the names of all children in the class, including half-timers, if any.

3 Each class containing children above and below the age of five years must have two registers, one for those above, the other for those below that age.[1]

The name of a child must be transferred from one of

[1] Minute of the Board of Education, July 7th, 1904.

these to the other not later than the end of the week in which he attains his fifth birthday."[1]

Registers for Special Classes.

"For any class in a subject for which a special grant is paid under the Code, or for any class in the ordinary subjects held in accordance with the time table elsewhere than at the school there must be a special register.

In these registers the dates of meetings and the times during which the scholar is under instruction at the meetings must be accurately shown."

The special classes refer to instruction in such subjects as cookery, laundry, dairy work, gardening, and handicrafts,[2] which are usually taught at centres.

Special Rules for Attendance Registers

1. "There must be columns for the admission numbers and names of the scholars, both of which must invariably be entered at the same time

There must be a column for the attendances at each meeting in the school year. Each of these columns should be properly dated before any entry of attendance or absence is made in it. The columns must be grouped in weeks, and at the foot of each there must be spaces for entering the total number of children present, when the minimum time constituting an attendance begins, and the total number withdrawn before the time constituting an attendance is complete

There must be spaces for recording the total attendances in the quarter made by each child

2 If school fees are entered in the register, they should be kept quite separate from the entries of attendances;

[1] Minute of the Board of Education, July 7th, 1904.
[2] See Art. 34, Code 1904.

the best place will be the extreme left of the page before the names of the scholars.

3. "The approved time table must provide adequate time at each meeting of the school for marking the registers, and this time must end before the commencement of the minimum time constituting an attendance.

The marking of the registers for the afternoon meeting may not commence within an hour of the close of the morning meeting, except on occasions for which the special sanction of the Board has been given to a shorter interval. This proceeding is very undesirable, but special cases may occur, such as those of country schools in the North during the winter, where there is good reason for making the afternoon meeting of the school follow the morning meeting after a short interval.

4. During the time set apart for registration at every meeting of the school—

Every scholar whose name has been entered in and not removed from the admission register must be marked (present) or ◯ (absent).

Just before the completion of the time set apart for registration the number of scholars marked present must be entered in the space provided, and to ensure accuracy a count of those actually present should be made before the number is recorded.

5. During the minimum time constituting an attendance—

The mark of presence of any scholar who leaves before completing an attendance must be cancelled at once by drawing a ring round it thus, ◯

But this need not be done in the case of a scholar leaving the school for instruction in a special class held outside the school, unless it is subsequently ascertained that such scholar has not completed the minimum time constituting an attendance.

Just before the completion of the minimum time—

The number of the scholars whose marks of attendance have been cancelled must be entered in the space provided

6 " Any scholar marked absent at any meeting who is found—when the registers of a central class for cookery, drawing science, etc , or the registers of attendance at museums or other approved places are examined—to have been present during the minimum time constituting an attendance at such class or partly at such class and partly at the school, may have the letter C, D, S, M, A, etc., entered inside the mark of absence, thus (c) (D) (s) (M) (A). All attendances so registered should be added to the total attendances of each child at some time not later than the end of the school year.

7 When a child is prevented from attending the school by reason of a notice of a sanitary authority under Article 56 of the Code, or any provision of an Act of Parliament, or is excluded under medical advice, his mark of absence should be entered thus, $(I.)$ (epidemic sickness)

8 When the school does not meet on an occasion for which space is provided in the registers, this space must before the next meeting be cancelled by one or more lines being plainly drawn through it The reason why the school did not meet should always appear in the log book For longer periods 'holiday' should be written across the column

9. The attendance registers must be marked every time the school meets, however small the attendance, and the meeting must be counted in ascertaining the average attendance

" N.B.—In country districts, where the children have to come from some distance to attend school, a meeting of the school may occasionally be abandoned without previous notice on days when, owing to inclement weather, the attendance is so small as seriously to interfere with the ordinary working of the school

In such a case, the children who reach the school so wet that sitting in school for the usual school hours is likely to be injurious to their health, should be sent home at once. The children not likely to be injured by remaining for the usual school hours may be admitted and allowed to receive instruction without the registers being marked or the meeting reckoned. Whenever this is done, full particulars of the circumstances must be entered in the log-book, and a record should be kept of the numbers sent home and retained in school respectively."

Rules for the use of the Half-time Register

10 " A separate register must be provided for half-time scholars. The name of no scholar should be entered in this unless he has obtained a labour certificate from the Local Authority of the district and is actually employed in conformity therewith.

11 At the close of each week, the number of the two-hour attendances made by each of the half-time scholars during the week must be ascertained from the class registers and posted in the half-time register.

12. At the end of the year a list must be drawn up and signed on behalf of the Local Authority, certifying (*a*) the number of two-hour attendances made by each half-time

scholar, (*b*) the addition claimed on his behalf. This addition may not exceed

> (i) *One-half* of the two-hour attendances made by the scholar during the year, or during the portion of the year that has elapsed since the scholar became qualified as a half-timer ; or
>
> (ii) Such a number as when added to the number of his two-hour attendances will give a total equal to *three-fourths* of the number of meetings of the school during the year, or during the portion of the year that has elapsed since the scholar became qualified as a half-timer."

Rules as to the Register of Summaries.

1. "All entries in the register of summaries, whether for a class or for the whole department, must be given separately for children below and above the age of five years [1]

2. At the close of each week or part of the week during which the school has been open the following entries must be made in the register of summaries in respect of that period—

> (1) The number of meetings of each department.
> (2) The total attendances of each class.
> (3) The total attendances of each department ; and
> (4) The average attendance of each department.

3. At the end of the school year the average attendance for the year should be ascertained for each section of a school or department for which a separate return is

[1] Minute of the Board of Education, July 7th, 1904.

necessary by dividing the total attendances made in that
year by the number of meetings of the corresponding
section of the school department. The average attendance
for children below and above the age of five years must be
separately ascertained [1]

4 "An entry must be made in the register of summaries
of the classification of the children of each sex according to
their ages on the last day of the school year."

Verification of the Registers

1 " The Managers are held responsible for the supervision and effective verification of the registration, and at
the end of the school year are required to certify—

   (1) that the registers have been accurately kept in
       accordance with the rules of this schedule; and
   (2) that the accuracy of the registers has been tested
       by the managers on several occasions and the
       result recorded in the log book

2 In order to be able to give this certificate Managers
are expected to visit the school without notice, at least once
in a quarter, to check the registration, at a time when the
class registers ought to have been closed by an entry of the
number of children present at the beginning of the
minimum time constituting an attendance "

Reference facilities will be increased by entering the
surnames first on the class and admission registers. In
the case of the class registers it is best, too, to arrange the
names in alphabetical order The greatest care should
be taken to see that these registers are *closed to time*, and
that the total number at the foot of the column corresponds with the number of children present It is usual
to indicate a punctual-attendance by a red mark and a

[1] Minute of the Board of Education, July 7th, 1904.

late attendance by a black one. In lieu of having the
class registers divided into four quarters, it is thought
that a three term division would be a more convenient
arrangement. Such registers are being introduced in
some districts Class registers should be preserved "at
least ten years."

Admission and summary registers "must never be
destroyed." The kind of information to be obtained from
the summary will be seen from the tabulated forms below.

WEEKLY RECORDS.

Class or Standard	Roll	Number present at all	Total Attendances	Percentage.	Week ended	No. present every morning and afternoon.
					Mon M. A.	
					Tues M. A	
					Wed. M. A.	
					Thur. M. A	
Totals					Fri. M. A	

QUARTERLY RECORDS (for the School as a whole)

Week ended	No. of times open		No. on Roll	No. present at all	Total Attendances
	M.	A.			
Totals or Averages for the Quarter.					

The yearly records include the following and also a table similar to the quarterly one, in which the corresponding numbers for the four quarters are set out and summarised to give the annual figures

	Years of age.	Nos.		Nos.
Total number of children on admission register on last day of school year	3 and under 4 4 ,, ,, 5 5 ,, ,, 6 6 ,, ,, 7 7 ,, ,, 8 8 ,, ,, 9 9 ,, ,, 10 10 ,, ,, 11 11 ,, ,, 12 12 ,, ,, 13 13 ,, ,, 14 14 ,, ,, 15 15 and over		No of scholars admitted during the year . .. No. of scholars left during the year . . . Average attendances for year .	
	Total			

Bye-law Returns

Bye-laws returns have, as a rule, to be made by teachers weekly, annually, and occasionally. The weekly returns usually consist of the attendances of each scholar made on a form which is a "duplicate" of the class register In some areas, however, the "ship" system has been introduced with great success. In this system, each scholar's name is entered on a separate "slip" of paper, whereon his attendances for a quarter are recorded week by week.

The annual return is of a more elaborate character and takes the form of a summary of attendances during the year for each department, chiefly based upon ages of the children. Occasional returns generally refer to individual scholars whose parents are about to be summoned before a magistrate for irregularity of attendance

Records of School Progress.

Records of school progress are necessary to satisfy the requirements of the Board of Education and many local education authorities, and are based on the educational year. To secure completeness in these records, it is desirable to furnish each class with three books (1) the progress and report book, printed forms of which can be obtained from most educational publishers, (2) an ordinary exercise book for the teacher to record briefly the work done week by week, (3) the teacher's note-book, intended mainly for such memoranda as involve due preparation of lessons

Most progress and report books are framed on the basis of quarterly or term examinations by the head teacher Assuming that term examinations are held, then each progress book should contain (1) For each term and each subject of instruction, a brief résumé of the work proposed to be done, together with a space for the head teacher's criticisms on each subject after the term's examination (2) A further space for each term in which the head teacher can summarise the value of the work done by the class as a whole under such general headings as (a) instruction, (b) discipline, (c) punctual and regular attendance (3) An individual schedule of the scholars on which may be shown the progress of each pupil in the various subjects (including conduct), that constitute the curriculum. (4) Blank sheets on which may be recorded the tests given at the examinations, and also the proposed syllabuses for the year

It is evident that syllabuses ought to be carefully prepared before the commencement of the year in which they are to be put into operation The head teacher's criticisms should be reasonably exhaustive, and aim at being especially helpful to the class teacher. Praise and condemnation should be fearlessly recorded as truth and justice demand

The progress book, as indicated here, ought only to apply to the upper classes in an infant school

The Child's Book

Many years ago the Board of Education instituted a "child's book," which contained most of the information now recorded in the admission register in connection with each scholar's name. This book was intended to be a complete record of the child's educational progress, and practically to become, when the time arrived, his leaving certificate. The "child's book" was, however, abandoned after a short trial. Some simple form of a child's book seems desirable. In the French schools[1] a book of this kind exists, for each scholar enrolled in a primary school receives a *cahier de devoirs mensuels*, or exercise book, in which he records the first lesson of each month during his school life. This has to be done entirely without aid. The purpose of this book is indicated thus in an official circular: "Une chose importe, et c'est la seule, qu'il existe dans toute école et pour tout enfant sans exception un cahier gardé avec soin, qui, d'une manière, ou d'une autre, et par un nombre suffisant de spécimens empruntés aux diverses époques de sa scolarité, puisse fournir au bout de quelques années une preuve irrécusable de la régularité de ses études et la trace de sa propre assiduité ou de ses absences."

P. T. Records

It is now essential to keep records of the work done by pupil teachers in the day schools. These records should

[1] See "Rural Education in France," by J. C. Medd, Special Reports, Vol. 7.

briefly indicate for each session (1) the time spent in
criticism lessons, and the classes or standards to which
such lessons were given ; (2) the time spent in work other
than actual teaching—the kind of work to be named and
the class or standard with which it was associated , (3) the
time spent in actual charge of a class, the size and grade
of the class being given , (4) work done as an aid to the
class teacher, and the time given thereto The conduct
and progress of the pupil teacher should be summed up
by the head teacher at the close of each quarter or term

   These records should be entered in a pupil teachers'
journal kept entirely for that purpose

Hygienic Records

   In Germany the school doctor has become a recognised
institution in the majority of the large towns   Berlin had
in 1901 a staff of ten medical practitioners to watch over
the schools, while Charlottenburg has one medical man
for every two schools   The doctor's duties vary a little
according to district, but generalised they may be said to
be .—

   (1) To examine every scholar as to condition of health
       · and to take his weight, height, chest and other
         measurements
   (2) To deal promptly with any suspected cases or
         conditions which concern the health of indi-
         vidual children or the school as a whole
   (3) To examine periodically the school buildings and
         report on any hygienic defects.
   (4) To examine children proposed for the special or
         defective schools

   In the Charlottenburg schools scholars are medically
classed as "under control" and "normal," the former

being examined periodically by the doctor and anthropo-
metric figures duly recorded, the latter by the teachers
taking measurements in the same way. The resultant
health schedules are carefully preserved.

Quite recently the central education authority of Germany decreed that *all* primary schools should be subject
to periodical medical inspection.[1]

In America child study departments, in which anthropo-
metric statistics are collected and tabulated, have been
established at a few large centres. A similar system of
weighing and measuring children has been adopted by a
branch of the Child Study Association at Liverpool. Sir
James Crichton Browne, M.D., urged in 1884 "the
systematic measurement of the children in all elementary
schools" as supplying "information of the highest
practical and scientific value."[2] The Medical Officer
(Education) of the London County Council also thinks
that something should be done in this direction.[3]

Ophthalmic Records

It is the practice in some educational areas in England
for the teacher annually to test the eyesight of the scholars
by means of charts supplied for that purpose. The records
of these tests are preserved and entered on the class
registers; the scholars arranged in the class accordingly;
and the oculist supplements the teacher's investigations
in all cases in which the vision is defective, and sends
"advice cards" to the parents. Serious defects in vision

[1] See Report of Mr. G. Andrew to the Scotch Education Department,
1904.

[2] See *Over-pressure in Elementary Schools*, 1884, and Report of the
Third International Congress for the Welfare and Protection of
Children, 1902.

[3] See Report of Medical Officer for the year ended March 1904.

are often caused by the habitual insufficiency of the distance of the scholar's eye from his work. From five to ten per cent of the children in public elementary schools suffer from defective vision. Nervousness, headaches, and fatigue are the result.

Aural Records.

By investigation[1] it has been found that from thirteen to thirty per cent. of children suffer from defective hearing in one or both ears. Mouth breathing, a heavy look, variable powers of hearing, general dulness, inattention and variable intelligence are the usual symptoms of deafness. In minor cases deafness becomes accentuated by a cold and varies in degree from other causes according to the general health. In instances like these, and also in the case of deafness in one ear only, defective hearing becomes difficult to detect by the teacher. Great vigilance and care are therefore necessary, for the moral effect of condemning children for disobedience or inattention when these are the natural outcome of sensory defect, temporary or permanent, is too evident to be named. Scholars apparently hopelessly dull and inattentive have been found, when the causes of deafness have been removed, to be very intelligent and obedient. It is desirable that the teacher should be ever watchful for defects of this kind and keep records of his observations. Some periodical system of testing aural defects, similar to that adopted for testing vision, appears to be necessary. This is done in Chicago.

Defectives' Records.

A form similar to that given below, signed by the teacher of the ordinary school which the child has been attending, has been found useful as the basis of records by the "special" teacher and the Medical Officer.

[1] See *Fundamentals of Child Study*, by E. A. Kirkpatrick, 1901.

DEFECTIVES ADMISSION FORM.[1]

1. Name of child ..   ..
2. Address in full   .   .
3. Date of birth   ..   ..
4. How long has the child attended
   (a) this School?
   (b) any other School?
5. What is the appearance of the child—Stupid or bright?
6. Is the child: 1. Obedient; 2. Mischievous; 3 Spiteful?
7. Are the habits of the child correct and cleanly?
8. Are the propensities of the child peculiar or dangerous?
9. What is the mental capacity of the child?
   1. Observation
   2. Imitation.
   3. Attention.
   4. Memory.
   5. Reading.
   6. Writing.
   7. Calculation.
   8. Colour.
   9. Special tastes.
10. Is the child affectionate or otherwise?
11. Has the child any moral sense?
12. Have you any other information bearing on the case?

Signed
School____ _____
Department_____
Date_____

[*Children* UNDER SIX EN *should not, as a rule, be nominated for admission to a Special School.*]

[1] In use in London (under the L.C.C.).

Thermometric Records.

Every central hall and each class-room should be supplied with a thermometer and the temperature taken and recorded at least twice a day. The best times for taking the temperature are considered to be at 10 a m. and 3.30 p m. It is well for these records to take the form of a quarterly chart, which ought to be hung in a conspicuous position on the class-room walls.

Board of Education Regulations as to School Records.

Every school must have —

(*a*) A diary or log book.

The log book should be stoutly bound and contain not less than 300 ruled pages. It must be kept by the head teacher, who should enter in it, from time to time, such events as the introduction of new books, apparatus, or courses of instruction, any plan of lessons approved by the Board, the visits of managers, absence, illness, or failure of duty on the part of any of the school staff, or any special circumstance affecting the school that may, for the sake of future reference or for any other reason, deserve to be recorded. No reflections or opinions of a general character are to be entered in the log book.

Entries in the log book should be made by the head teacher at the end of each school week, and at such other times as occasion may require. No entries should be made by other persons except by the correspondent, by the managers who check the registers periodically, and by the inspector.

The log book should contain an explanation of the reason for the closing of the school on all occasions on which it is closed. It should also contain an account of all important variations in the attendance, and all deviations from the ordinary routine of the school.

(*b*) A book for recording minutes of managers' meetings.

(*c*) A portfolio to contain official letters.

(*d*) The Code of the Board of Education in force for the time being.

(*e*) A punishment book.

School Conference Records.

As long intervals often separate school conference meetings, it is desirable that the minutes should be entered in the book kept for that purpose, within a few days of a conference, and signed then by the head teachers of the various departments who were present. It is needless to say that the minutes should be of a purely formal character, but sufficiently wide in the absence of unanimity to cover expressed individual opinions.

The Three Years

For purposes of records and other matters there are three different years associated with every school, viz, the calendar year, for certificates of exemption by attendance, the school year, for finance and annual returns to the Board of Education; and the educational year, at the commencement of which most of the great changes in organisation and promotion of scholars are made

CHAPTER VI.

THE SCHOOL PREMISES IN CONNECTION WITH ORGANISATION.

Educational Effect of Good Premises.

SUITABLE rules for the planning and equipment of schools have been drawn up by the Board of Education for the guidance of local authorities These rules represent a minimum of requirements, and apply to all new buildings unless it is made clear that exceptions should be allowed.

The educational effect of good premises is undoubted. A simple, dignified, and, if possible, artistic exterior, suggestive of the purpose for which the building exists, is calculated, apart from other considerations, to make the scholars proud of their connection with the school, and to exercise a constant and impressive influence in the neighbourhood concerning the ideals of education

A really artistic school building—and it can be artistic in simplicity—radiates its beauty day and night It is a permanent expression of spiritual things ; it is sculptured stone and masonry embodying a great aim ; it is a silent power for good to all who look upon it, or dwell within the spell of its presence In poor and squalid neighbourhoods such a building is in its effects like a miniature sun that never sets. One might properly say to the local authorities, " Costly thy *buildings* as thy purse can buy, but not expressed in fancy."

It is an architectural canon that the exterior of a building should suggest the character of the interior, and the interior should of course be planned for, and adapted to, the work it is proposed to do. First and foremost the building must be planned in conformity with hygienic law. The child's extreme susceptibility to injury from a noxious environment demands that this shall be the primary consideration. The building should be so situated that the sun can reach all its classrooms without filtering through foliage or being obstructed by house-tops, that the air may be able freely to play round it, and that the natural drainage can be effected without saturating the sub-soil with moisture. It is well, too, to have the building standing back some distance from the main arteries of traffic, so that the work may not be disturbed by external sounds.

There should be a commodious playground, evenly warmed and well lighted rooms, and a thorough system of ventilation. Other considerations are the number of entrances and exits, a sufficiency of cloak-room accommodation, the number and distribution of class-rooms, facilities for adequate supervision and for the speedy passage of the pupils from one part of the building to another.

It is evident that the interior of a building will, if suitably planned, give material aid to the work of organisation, and assist in many ways to produce the best educational results. Pupils cannot be expected to work and develop according to their natural tendencies and abilities unless good light, fresh air, and change of position and of exercise daily and hourly companion their studies. Unless the body has a healthy environment and facilities for development, there is a tendency for the intellectual forces to wane and for the moral power to deteriorate.

Desirability of a Single View in Planning.

From the nature of the work to be accomplished and the large number of children that must be duly classified and

instructed, it is clearly desirable that a building to be used
as a school-house should be specially designed for that
purpose and that purpose only Too often in the past a
structure erected primarily as a hall for evening meetings
has been considered good enough for the education of children, without those temporary means of separating class
from class which are now deemed necessary to efficiency

The Small School.

There are, however, cases in which a single school-room
or small hall becomes a necessity. In many sparsely populated distincts there are village schools numbering from
twenty to fifty pupils representing probably almost as many
grades of attainments as are to be found in much larger urban
schools Small schools like these are generally organised
and taught by one certificated teacher It is, therefore, a
practical necessity of the situation to have all the pupils in
one room, so that while the teacher is giving oral instruction to one or more sections he may have the remainder
under supervision In cases of this kind a separate class-
room would be next to useless unless it accommodated the
whole of the scholars It would then be useful as giving
an opportunity of change and fresh air. A single-roomed
school should not exceed 600 square feet in floor space [1]

The Ordinary Graded School.

The best type of building, so far as interior arrangements
are concerned, is one with a central hall, and the class-
rooms opening into it, each room with its independent
entrance

Schools or departments under one head teacher are
usually graded according to their recognised official

[1] See Board of Education Rules.

accommodation, or habitual attendance. An example is
given below

Grade i	accommodation	under 200.
Grade ii	"	200 to 300
Grade iii	"	300 to 400.
Grade iv	"	400 to 600
Grade v	"	above 600

The Hall

The hall is common ground for all the classes. If used
as an ordinary class-room, permanently or temporarily,
such use throws a great burden on the teachers, subtracts
from the efficiency of the work, and seriously interferes
with the purposes for which a hall is primarily intended.
The hall should, of course, be sufficiently large to accommodate all the children in the department of which it forms
a part, and be as well warmed, lighted, and ventilated as
the other parts of the building.

It occasionally happens that a central hall has to serve
for the joint use of two departments. The Board of Education raises no objection to this provided it is reasonably
accessible to all the scholars. Sometimes this joint use
causes much inconvenience to the department the class-
rooms of which open directly into the hall. The hall,
besides the great general advantages that it confers, is
particularly useful for physical training in the winter
months, and at all other periods of the year when open air
space is not available. The hall must not be included in
the accommodation, except as a temporary measure, and
then only by special sanction of the Board of Education.

The Class-Rooms.

The number of class-rooms must be determined by the
accommodation of the department. Generally one room

for every fifty scholars is a fairly satisfactory arrangement.
No class-room ought to accommodate less than thirty pupils
on the ten square feet basis The Board of Education
Regulations, which have to be framed to meet every variety
of circumstance, limit the size of a class-room to sixty
children, " but in special cases somewhat larger rooms may
be approved " It is not desirable to have all the rooms of
the same size, since the lower classes are generally the
largest In a department accommodating, say, 320 children
a suitable distribution of places would be found in seven
class-rooms with the following accommodations—40, 40,
40, 48, 48, 50, 54, or 35, 40, 45, 48, 48, 50, 54 A well-
balanced school of three departments—boys', girls', and
infants'—would be represented by the respective accommodations of 320, 320, 350

Class-rooms that must be used as a means of reaching
any other part of the building, public thoroughfare, or
playground—" passage rooms," as they are called—are not
satisfactory, as interruption of work and strain on the
teacher's powers, especially his patience, are involved It
is important, when class-rooms are separated by movable
partitions, that the separation should be reasonably complete both as regards sight and sound It is often found
convenient in emergency and other cases to be able to
convert two class-rooms into one A room that accommodates seventy children, for example, which is too large for
one teacher, could be suitably divided into two parts of
thirty and forty for the use of the upper standards, and be
re-converted into its original size as occasion requires.

(1) *Movable Partitions*

In some of the older school buildings, containing only
one or two large rooms, collapsible partitions of a substantial kind, glazed in their upper parts, have been found

an effective means of creating class-room accommodation, while still retaining the advantage of being able to restore the rooms to their original sizes when desired. This kind of partition effects a complete separation from floor to ceiling, and is easily folded like a drawing-room screen, its support strains being chiefly borne by the lateral walls to which it is permanently attached. By these means a hall becomes converted into two, three or more class-rooms according to the number of partitions, and can still be used as a hall for assembly, dismissal, and other purposes. This arrangement, however, has its disadvantages, often in the ill-shaped class-rooms, and the need of independent entrances and exits; but the gain, in other respects, is very considerable.

(2) *Curtains, etc.*

The use of curtains to separate one part of a room from another has some advantages. Curtains are, perhaps, less objectionable when made of washing material; but they almost invariably obstruct the light and do very little towards deadening the sound. Dwarf portable screens of wood and cathedral glass are sometimes used instead of curtains.

Class-rooms of the same superficial area and of equal height are not necessarily suitable for the same number of children. The kind of desks and the possibilities of arranging them satisfactorily in regard to the light, etc., the position of the doors, heating apparatus or fire-places, the shape of the room, etc., are factors for consideration in determining the accommodation. As to shape, the Board of Education expresses approval of a room approximating to that of a square.

(3) *The Extra Room*

Besides the desirability of each room in a department having a marginal accommodation, there is need for an occasional or extra room, which should not be reckoned in the official accommodation Such a room could be put to a variety of uses, all pointing in the direction of increased efficiency It might, too, assume many forms according to local needs It might be, for example, utilised as an ungraded room either permanently or intermittently If permanently, the room should be a comparatively small one, if intermittently, it ought to be of sufficient size to accommodate any of the ordinary classes

On the other hand, a demonstration room is most useful —especially for the science work of the upper standards or the object-lessons of the lower ones, and for lantern lessons generally A room of this kind is usually fitted with a well-equipped demonstration table or bench ; a double vertically sliding blackboard, the framework of which is fixed to the wall nearest the table and facing the class , and also with such terraced flooring that each row of desks rises above the one in front of it, giving every scholar an easy and uninterrupted view of any experiment that is being performed. It is not uncommon to have a smooth white surface of cement behind the sliding blackboard, to take lantern pictures The Board of Education will not, however, approve of a special lecture-room of this kind, outside the accommodation, in any *ordinary* public elementary school. Apart from the visual facilities which a room of this kind confers, the opportunity for occasional change that it affords is one that promotes both bodily health and mental alertness.

With certain exceptions, every class-room ought to be stepped Usually three rows of stepping are deemed sufficient

(1) *Science and Art Rooms.*

So far class-rooms for ordinary purposes have been considered. There is in educational circles a growing demand for other specially designed and equipped rooms, suitable for practical science and instruction in drawing. For example, a minute of the London County Council under date of July 1904 reads thus :

"We have had under consideration the question of the provision of science and drawing class-rooms in ordinary public elementary L.C.C. schools, together with a suggestion of the Board of Education that the Council should consider whether science rooms and drawing class-rooms should form part of the equipment of a public elementary school.

"After fully considering the matter we are of opinion that science rooms and drawing class-rooms should be provided in all new public elementary schools. In coming to this conclusion we have been influenced by educational as well as financial considerations. With reference to the question of educational efficiency, we are of opinion that the matter should be considered from the triple standpoint of mental, physical and moral training. Upon this question we would point out—(1) that it is most important that a child should recognise that his school education has a direct bearing upon every department of life ; that this can be but imperfectly secured when nearly the whole of his time after leaving the infants' school is devoted to learning from books or by oral instruction ; that it is of importance that throughout the whole of his school career he should be taught to observe with care, to work with accuracy, and to reason with intelligence from his own observations, under the guidance of trained teachers ; (2) that the training of hand and eye by careful experimental work in a properly fitted science room, or by drawing, painting, and modelling in a suitably equipped art room, furnished with examples affording inspiration to the young pupil, is as important a branch of physical culture as the physical exercises required of all pupils in a public elementary school, (3) that the moral effect of training in accurate measurement, in exact workmanship, and particularly in carrying out simple quantitative experiments the results of which can be tested by independent methods is of incalculable value in the formation of character.

" In order to secure the results indicated we are of opinion that it is of great importance, if not absolutely necessary, that a school should be provided with rooms furnished otherwise than as ordinary class-rooms, for the amount of freedom which such rooms afford to the pupils in their work greatly reduces the sense of strain, and consequent fatigue, which is incidental to continuous work at the school desk.

" From the financial point of view, the provision of rooms for teaching science and art, in the roof of a large school building, involves little more additional cost than that required for the extension of the stairs and the provision of a fire-proof floor in place of an ordinary ceiling ; while the rooms which can thus be provided, though eminently suitable for the purposes indicated, are not well adapted for use as ordinary class-rooms.

" The syllabuses of instruction will comprise the use of simple measuring instruments, and the representation, by graphic methods, of the results obtained, the simplest experiments in mechanics, physics and chemistry, and observations and experiments bearing upon ' nature study,' as illustrating those natural laws which most conspicuously affect every-day life, and which may consequently be expected to appeal to every child.

" We are of opinion that the Board of Education should be informed that, for the reasons stated, the Council con-

siders the provision of science rooms and drawing class-
rooms to be necessary for the educational efficiency of
public elementary schools."

(5) *Infant Rooms.*

All rooms for infants must be on the ground floor, the
means of access to which should, as a rule, be independent
of those for the senior children   In village areas, where it
is not uncommon to find infant classes in the same department with the older scholars, separate entrances are not
always practicable   A hall or some free space for march-
ing and games is essential to an infant department or
infant classes   There is a division of opinion among
teachers and other educational experts as to the value for
the youngest children in infant departments of flat floors
on the one hand, and stepped flooring on the other   Up
to the present it has been a general practice to provide
galleries for the babies   Some teachers prefer flat floors
and kindergarten desks for these tiny ones, while others
place their faith in the value of the gallery   The gallery,
though exceedingly useful in many ways, especially if so
arranged that the teacher can easily get behind each child,
is yet open to the objection that the stepping causes the
children occasionally to fall

Some babies' rooms are arranged so that the seats or
kindergarten desks are placed around the three sides, and
thus most of the floor space is available for exercises and
games   In this case all the floor space is flat   There
seems to be little doubt that the flat floor is best for
children up to five years of age

Again, it has been advocated that the best relative
positions for teacher and taught are for the former to be
on a platform and the latter on the flat   This arrangement is objectionable, since it causes the children to raise

their eyes above the horizontal, and this throws a strain on the levator muscle which it is not well adapted to bear [1]

When practicable, a nature study room for the infants is very desirable. If this is not possible, inside ledges to the windows, whereon seeds and plants may be developed, are a fairly good substitute. Each class-room, indeed, ought to be a miniature nature study room in itself.

A suitable height for a class-room is 13 ft. Any height over that is considered waste

(6) *Accommodation of Rooms*

A large number of schools still have their accommodation reckoned on the 8 sq. ft. basis, *i.e.* the superficial area necessary for each child In all new schools the Board of Education is demanding a 10 sq ft. basis for senior departments and 9 sq ft. for infants A central hall, and rooms for cookery, laundry, manual training for boys, science and drawing, must not be included in the official accommodation

Entrances, Staircases, and Corridors

There should be separate entrances and staircases for each department and sex The chief entrances must not be through cloakrooms, and all entrance doors should be made, for obvious reasons, to open both ways, namely inwardly and outwardly Fireproof staircases in which there are no triangular steps are necessary Staircases should be sufficient in number and breadth to provide for cases of emergency, and upper floors that exceed 250 in accommodation should have a second staircase

Classes ought always to be marched in single or double file, under careful supervision, both from the playground

[1] See Report of the Medical Officer of the late School Board for London for the year ended March 1904.

to the class-rooms and from the class-rooms to the play-ground. Accidents are apt to occur unless steadiness is observed in descending a staircase. Corridors or staircases should never be used, even for temporary purposes, for storage of any kind.

Cloakrooms and Lavatories

Cloakrooms should have double doorways, so that scholars may enter by one door and leave by another. They should not be passage rooms, nor directly connected with any rooms used for teaching purposes. Thorough ventilation is essential. There should, at least, be one peg for every child in the school. There is a disposition in many boys' departments to ignore the cloakroom in fine weather. This ought never to be allowed. Considerations of health forbid this disuse.

One lavatory basin for about every fifty children is considered desirable. The absence of proper accommodation of this kind is not only mischievous in its direct effects, but also in its ultimate tendencies. As personal cleanliness is of the utmost importance, it ought to be regarded as one of the chief lessons to be learnt in school life. It is well, therefore, for the school to begin this lesson by providing suitable lavatory accommodation.

Lighting

Dark corners or dark places of any kind are harmful. As regards class-rooms, left lighting is best, that is, light directly striking the scholars' left shoulders when facing the teacher. Supplementary windows are, however, often necessary for ventilating purposes. When left lighting is impracticable, right lighting should be secured, if possible. The Board of Education does not approve of sky-lights except for halls. Lighting that comes mainly from behind

the scholars or immediately in front of them is of the
worst kind

Interior colouring has a not unimportant bearing on the
lighting. The colours and tints used for walls, ceilings,
and fittings ought to be restful to the eyes In some
areas teachers are advised in good time of the intention to
repaint the school and requested to suggest the interior
colouring. With the aid of artistic friends, it sometimes
happens that the happiest choice is made.

In recent buildings, in accordance with the Board of
Education Regulations, the windows are large and
numerous, and reach nearly to the ceiling It is necessary
that not less than one-fifth of the wall space be occupied
by windows The "dim religious light" may be produc-
tive of sentiment, but it is inimical to health when associated
with schools

Assuming that rooms are adequately provided with
openings, it is extremely important that the glass be kept
clean, otherwise the passage of light to the rooms will not
only be seriously obstructed, but the dirt deposited on the
glass may prove injurious to the health of the children.
In any case, such deposits necessarily lower the vital
properties of the air, and may, if one pupil in the class is
suffering from incipient disease, be the means of causing
infection

Heating and Ventilation.

Heating and ventilation are inextricably involved and
must be considered together Good ventilation consists in
driving foul air out of the room as soon as created, and re-
placing it, without causing draughts, by fresh air containing
normal quantities of oxygen This seems a very simple
matter, but it has proved to be one of the most difficult of all

problems. There appears to be no doubt that many school-rooms are poorly ventilated even when reasonable use is made of the appliances available. The *odor scholasticus*, especially during the winter season, is only too evident. Besides the ordinary means of ventilating by open windows, Tobin's tubes, chimney extractors, wall and ceiling gratings, and open fire-places have so far failed to give that adequate and continuous supply of fresh air which is desirable. Tobin's tubes, generally placed in corners of rooms, are a valuable means of inlet, while separate air chimneys are serviceable in providing for the outflow of foul air containing such deleterious impurities as carbon dioxide and albuminoid ammonia.

Generally town air contains four parts of carbon dioxide (CO_2) to every 10,000 parts. An atmosphere that contains about ten parts in 10,000 is injurious to health. It has been found by experiment that carbonic acid gas takes up the space of fifteen or more parts in 10,000 in some school class-rooms just before the recreation interval—and this, too, when reasonable use has been made of the means of ventilation at hand. Haldane's apparatus is able to record the amount of CO_2 impurity in a room any time during the day.

It is a singular fact that children give out from their bodies proportionately a larger quantity of organic impurities than adults. These impurities, ordinarily consisting of the tiniest particles of epithelium and fatty matters, together with CO_2, etc., ought to find a ready means of exit from the rooms, otherwise these small organic particles get deposited on the walls and their ledges -especially if the walls are cold—and make demands upon the oxygen of the rooms that is needed for other purposes. The *odor scholasticus* is mainly due to these organic substances in the air.

The tendency to deposit on the school walls shows the

desirability (1) of never allowing the walls to get abnormally cold even during the night, since they take a comparatively long time to get restored to the temperature of the room's atmosphere again, and (2) of ventilating the premises thoroughly immediately after the morning and afternoon sessions. Lofty rooms, though they give extra cubic space, do not help to maintain a good atmosphere or to promote sound ventilation. Indeed, it is considered that a height above 13 ft may prove baneful unless the openings are correspondingly high.

Good ventilation should provide, at least, 3,000 cubic feet of fresh air per hour for every child and not allow air to stagnate in any part of the building. It should further provide that the admitted air be approximately of the same temperature as that which is in the room, for when the air is warmed before admission it prevents draughts. This can to a great extent be effected by means of modern appliances. The Plenum system of ventilation claims to do all this. It drives the warm air into the rooms near the ceiling and draws out the foul air on the same side of the room near the floor. In this way every room can have a renewed atmosphere from eight to ten times in an hour.

When, however, natural ventilation, as distinguished from mechanical ventilation like the Plenum system, is adopted, the windows should be used as the chief outlets for foul air in the cold season; they should also be used as inlets when the air temperature external to the school is not much lower than that within.

The value of the recreation interval from the ventilation point of view only, is great. As soon as the room is cleared all doors and windows should be opened, so that the children may return to an atmosphere as pure as that in the playground.

Heating and ventilation depend on one another. Heating is ventilation's motive power. Heating is effected by (1) open fires or closed stoves, (2) warm air, (3) hot-water pipes; or, taking a scientific principle of classification, by (1) radiation and (2) propulsion. Convection, of course, plays an important part in all systems of ventilation. Galton's grate, which is largely used, has a warm-air chamber behind it. The chamber draws the cold air from the outside, and, after warming it, discharges it into the room through gratings.

The temperature in an infants' school ought not to be allowed to fall below 60° F, while that for the senior scholars might vary from 56° to 60° F. In no case ought the temperature to fall below 50° or to rise above 60°, that is, of course, if it lies within human power of control. When the temperatures of the air inside and outside a school differ by 10° F, a draught will be caused unless precautions are taken.

In summer time, when the heat is great, sprinkling the floor occasionally with water helps to keep the temperature down.

Each class-room should be furnished with a thermometer.

The Board of Education considers an open fire and a temperature of 60° essential for babies' rooms. The Board only approves of stoves "with proper chimneys and supplied with fresh air direct from the outside." Further, stoves must not "become red-hot or otherwise contaminate the air," and must be so placed as not to interfere with "floor space necessary for teaching purposes."

All fireplaces and stoves should be furnished with fireguards.[1]

[1] On the subject of ventilation the student is referred to Carpenter's *School Hygiene* (Certificate Edition); *School Hygiene*, by Newsholme and

Sanitary Arrangements [1]

Scholars' latrines should be in the playgrounds and completely separated, and if possible well removed, from the main school building. They should, of course, together with their approaches, be quite distinct for boys and girls. Offices not provided with either automatic or individual means of flushing should be flushed at least twice a day by the caretaker. It is essential to have a full and ready supply of wholesome water for drinking purposes.

Desks

The rules of the Board of Education in reference to desks may be thus summarised : (1) Seats and desks, with backs to them, must be provided for all scholars, suitable to their ages, and must be arranged at right angles to the window wall. (2) Each scholar should be allowed at least eighteen inches, and there should be gangways of eighteen inches between groups of desks and between groups and walls. (3) Desks should not be longer than twelve feet, and not more than six rows deep. (4) In the case of long desks, the teacher must be able to pass between the rows, and in the case of dual desks, behind the back rows. (5) An inclination or slope of 15° for each desk is sufficient. Flat top desks[2] are objectionable. For writing purposes the " distance " should be zero. (The " distance " is zero when a vertical line from the inner edge of the desk exactly meets the inner edge of the seat. When the seat goes

Pakes ; and the Report of the Medical Officer (School Board for London) for the year ended March 1901.

[1] See Board of Education Rules for the Planning and Fitting up of Public Elementary Schools.

[2] This does not apply to kindergarten desks.

beyond that line, or does not reach it, the "distance" is respectively *minus* and *plus*.)

Usually desks are made in six sizes, graduated to meet the needs of scholars of various ages. It is generally considered desirable to have the zero "distance." The use of the flap in dual desks should not be neglected. The flap is not only valuable for reading purposes, but also for giving freer play to the body during oral lessons. It further enables the scholars to stand comfortably erect without leaving the desk.

(1) *Dangers from Improper Desks.*

The importance of having desks to meet the needs of each scholar has not yet been sufficiently recognised. Spinal deformity, cramped chests, short-sightedness, eye strain, and stooping habits are, among other evils, the outcome of compelling children to sit for hours daily in desks unsuited to their physical proportions.

Preference must be given to the dual, rather than to the long desk. The single desk, largely used in the United States, is again better than the dual desk. The use of the single desk, however, considerably reduces the accommodation of a room—by about twenty-five per cent.—and the Board of Education will only approve of its use under exceptional circumstances; as, for example, in the first class of a school, where the single locker desk has been found very convenient.

(2) " *Sheffield System.*"

The "Sheffield System" of desks is in favour in many schools in the North of England. In this system the desk is long and accommodates six pupils, but the seats are isolated and screwed, like the desk itself, to the floor. It is claimed[1] for this system that every pupil is easily accessible,

[1] See Report of Medical Officer (School Board for London 1904.

that the lateral space between the seats enables the pupil to stand—so that drill, for example, may be taken—that it becomes impracticable to overcrowd a room, and that it facilitates the sweeping and washing of floors.

General Conditions for Good Desking.

In order that each child may be accommodated with a desk suitable to its needs, it is necessary (1) That desks should be made in a greater number of sizes than at present. (2) That each child in a class having found a

The "Sheffield" System, showing an isolated seat for each scholar.

suitable desk, should be allowed to retain it for six months, when seats should be redistributed. Some children grow so rapidly that a year ought not to be allowed to intervene between each redistribution. (3) Each class-room or class should be supplied at least with three different sizes of desks.[1] Age is but a small criterion of the physical proportions of children.

[1] That is for Senior Departments. Probably two sizes of desks would suffice for the lower grades of an Infant School.

It is especially desirable that the desk should allow of the regulation distance between the eyes and the object in desk-work This varies from ten to sixteen inches

It is not possible to secure these conditions with the ordinary long desk or with that associated with the "Sheffield system,' the seats not being adjustable. It is evident that if the *seats* of desks, which should never be flat but always slightly concave, were made adjustable, a much larger number of desk sizes would not be needed, and the necessity for a periodical redistribution of seats would not be so pressing Height of children is not always a guide in selecting suitable desks for them Any two scholars, for example, of the same height might be taken, and they would probably be found to differ in length of trunk, legs and arms, all of which are factors in determining suitability of desks. Girls, too, differ in this respect from boys, for they have generally longer bodies and shorter limbs It is important, too, for teachers to know that from twelve to fourteen years of age girls grow much more rapidly than boys

In Lucerne, experiment has shown the desirability of having from five to seven different sizes of desks for each class In Chicago, measurement of children proves the necessity for supplying each school with five different sizes of stationary desks and three sizes of adjustable desks The Child Study Committee[1] has, therefore, recommended that each class or grade be supplied with from 75 to 85 per cent of stationary desks suitable to the physical proportions of children generally found in a particular grade, and also from 15 to 25 per cent of adjustable desks

Most scholars take up the forward sitting position which usually results from improper desks, and especially those that have the *plus* "distance." The tendencies of this position are to impede circulation, weaken the eyes, cause muscular strain and fatigue, and in the course of time even spinal curvature [1]

Infant Furniture

Flat floors have already been advocated for infants up to five years of age. Kindergarten dual desks are fairly suitable for such children, but a better arrangement appears to be the provision of low tables, at which, seated on miniature chairs, from eight to twelve children can find accommodation. This distribution of a class into small parties, together with the homely suggestiveness of tables and chairs, helps to encourage the social instinct and to excite self-expression. This arrangement is particularly beneficial to timid and nervous children. The supervision of the teacher and accessibility to the scholars are rather improved than otherwise by this plan for kindergarten instruction. With the chair the child has a freedom of movement that is most desirable at this age. Change of position obviates fatigue, fatigue creates fretfulness and lessens memory power. The sunshine of happiness is best for growth and development physically, morally, and intellectually. The face to back positions necessitated by groups of desks discourage the social sentiment and really isolate scholars through sitting together and forming the same class.

Wall Boards

It is well for infant class-rooms to have a composition wall board—chocolate colour is probably the best—within easy reach on every side. Many schools have this arrangement for free-arm drawing; in others, small blackboards are fixed to the walls of halls and of one or more class-rooms.

[1] See Child Study Report (No. 3) 1900-01, Chicago Public Schools. See also Burgerstein's *Schulhygiene.*

Some schools, too, take their free-arm drawing in desks by means of wire easels affixed thereto, into each of which fits a large millboard. The easily cleansable composition strip is, however, probably the best for very young children, especially as it enables them to stand whilst drawing

Blackboards, etc

Wall slates, in addition to the ordinary blackboards and easels, are a desirable acquisition to every class-room Such fixed slates are especially valuable for information which it is desired to keep before the eyes of the class for some time It is well known that the larger the number of senses that can be appealed to, the greater is the general educational effect and the stronger is the mental image created thereby. This, of course, has an important bearing on memory The audio-visual memory, for example, is stronger than either the auditory or visual taken separately Again, the audio-visual-articulatory memory is stronger than the audio-visual one, and so on [1] Blackboards in combination with wall slates often obviate the necessity for eye-straining on the part of the scholars

Every class-room should have its own cupboard for current stock Cupboards built into wall recesses give generally a neater appearance to a room than those not so fixed

Every school ought to have a First Aid equipment, proper accommodation for ink trays, and a museum cupboard, the last-named to contain only such objects as are likely to be generally useful in illustrating lessons This cupboard should not, therefore, as it sometimes is, be used for a collection of curiosities that are rarely moved from their positions, and occupy space that could

[1] See Child Study Report 1900-01, Chicago Public Schools

be better filled by really serviceable objects. It is well to encourage the scholars to assist in furnishing a cupboard of this kind

It is scarcely necessary to add that every infant department should have a complete kindergarten equipment.

The Teachers' Room

School premises can hardly be considered complete without a teachers' room, comfortably furnished and adequately supplied with lounge chairs. As the teachers' work is of an arduous nature an easy means of rest should be assured when not on active duty

Premises for Special Purposes.

The following are additional regulations[1] of the Board of Education concerning (1) the higher elementary school, (2) centres for special purposes, such as cookery, etc., (3) drawing and science rooms, and (4) schools for defectives

(1) *The Higher Elementary School.*

For a higher elementary school accommodating from 300 to 350 scholars, ten class-rooms will generally be required, since every class should have its own room, and no room should accommodate more than forty scholars

> (*a*) (i) The class-rooms may be furnished with single or dual desks as may be desired. Single desks should be two feet long, arranged in pairs with intervals of two inches and gangways of two feet
>
> (ii) If single desks are adopted, a class-room should have an area of about sixteen square feet per scholar. Class-rooms fitted with dual desks need not be so large, but a

[1] Extracted from the *Rules for the planning and fitting up of Public Elementary Schools*, etc.

minimum of about thirteen square feet per scholar will be required.

(b) Every higher elementary school should be provided with suitable laboratories.

(i) The laboratory accommodation must be sufficient to provide at one time for the largest class in the school.

(ii) There should generally be one laboratory for chemistry and one for physics

(iii) A laboratory should afford thirty square feet of floor space for each scholar, the minimum size will therefore be 600 square feet, but it is as a rule desirable that the laboratory should be somewhat larger. If, however, the laboratory accommodates more than twenty-five scholars a second teacher would be required.

(iv) Laboratories must be fitted with suitable tables, which must be well lighted; they should be properly supplied with gas and water. For chemical laboratories, sinks, cupboards, and the necessary fume closets must be provided.

(v) A small balance room may be provided if desired.

(c) (i) In addition to the class-rooms and laboratories a higher elementary school may include a lecture-room, which should be fitted with (1) a demonstration-table furnished with a gas and water supply and a sink, and (2) a fume closet A lecture-room should have an area of about 750 square feet.

(ii) If no separate lecture-room is provided, each of the class-rooms used by the third and fourth years should be fitted with a simple demonstration table

(iii) A small preparation room, fitted with bench, sink, cupboard and shelves, and proper supply of gas should be provided in a convenient position

(d) A drawing class-room for the more advanced drawing is desirable It should provide thirty square feet of floor space for each scholar; the best size will be a room with an area of 750 square feet If suitably lighted, the hall would answer for this purpose

(e) Other special rooms for cookery, laundry-work and manual instruction should be provided

(f) A higher elementary school should be planned with a central hall, but no class, other than drawing, can be recognised in such a hall

Rooms for Cookery, Manual Instruction, etc.

As a rule a single room for cookery, or laundry-work, or manual instruction, or science, or drawing, will serve for more than one school if provided as a centre in a convenient position Every such centre should have its own lavatory and cloak-room.

Large schools, or schools of an exceptional type, may sometimes require special rooms for their exclusive use.

(2) *Cookery*

A cookery room should be capable of accommodating twelve to eighteen at practice or thirty-six to fifty-four at demonstration at any one time The larger size will require 750 superficial feet and 10,500 cubic feet Provision for instruction in scullery work is necessary

The sink should be placed in full view of the teacher and children, and should be fitted with a cold water supply and a waste pipe.

There should also be a gallery or raised platform with desks to accommodate thirty-six to fifty-four children, according to the size of the room.

The floor space for practical work should afford about twenty square feet for each scholar, and should not be encumbered with desks, cupboards, or stoves.

In cookery rooms the ventilation needs special arrangements. Where a gas stove is used, it may be necessary to have a pipe fixed to carry off noxious fumes. The temperature should not be allowed to rise above seventy degrees.

The apparatus for lessons in cookery should include such stoves and other appliances as are usually found in the homes of the children.

(3) *Laundry.*

A laundry should be of simple construction, and entirely apart from the ordinary school buildings.

The proper size for a laundry is about 750 square feet. It should have a gallery or raised platform with desks for forty-two children.

Laundry tables should be large enough to allow at least three feet of space for each child when ironing.

The ventilation of rooms for laundry-work needs special arrangements for the removal of steam.

(4) *Housewifery.*

A housewifery centre[1] usually consists of an ordinary five- or six-roomed cottage such as the average parent of a

---

[1] The Board of Education has not, up to the present, laid down rules for the planning and fitting up of housewifery centres.

child attending an elementary school would occupy. It is, therefore, furnished simply and comfortably, and with such household appliances as are deemed necessary to efficient domestic management

(5) *Manual Instruction for Boys.*

In its plan, arrangements, construction, lighting, and ventilation, a manual instruction room should be modelled on a workshop rather than on a school. The construction should accordingly be simple. The roof may be either of lean-to or other ordinary form, according to circumstances. Its height at the windows in front of the benches need not be more than ten feet. The light must be ample. The temperature should not be so high as in an ordinary class-room. A flat ceiling is not, as a rule, necessary. Ample ventilation should be provided by inlets at a height of five feet from the floor, and by outlets at the highest point. A manual instruction room for twenty scholars should have a floor space of about 700 square feet.

(6) *Science Room.*

A room suitably fitted for elementary practical work in science may be provided for the use of one large or several contributory schools. Such a science room should not, as a rule, contain more than 600 square feet of floor space. It should be fitted with strong and plain tables, sinks, cupboards, and shelves, and where necessary, a fume closet. A proper supply of gas is necessary.

In addition to a science room, one of the ordinary class-rooms may be fitted with a simple demonstration-table and gas and water supply. But a special lecture-room cannot be approved in an ordinary public elementary school.

(7) Art Rooms

A drawing class-room can only be sanctioned where it is likely to be used for a reasonable time every week by the scholars from one large or several contributory schools. A suitable size for such a room is 600 square feet of floor space. Light should be admitted at a suitable height and angle from the north, north-east or east.

(8) Rooms for Defective Children

N.B.—These rules must be read in conjunction with the general rules for the planning and fitting up of public elementary schools.

(1) DAY SCHOOLS OR CLASSES FOR DEFECTIVE CHILDREN.

(*a*)[1] Twenty square feet of floor space per child in average attendance must be provided in the class-rooms. No class-room should contain less than 400 square feet of floor space.

(*b*)[1] All playgrounds, offices, cloakrooms, lavatories, entrances, and passages must be so constructed as to admit of easy supervision by the teacher of the school or class for defective children, and must, as a rule, be kept for the sole use of the children attending that school or class.

(*c*) All rooms for physically defective children must be on the ground floor.

(*d*) Where the premises are intended for the use of more than one class, they must, as a rule, include a wide and well-lighted corridor or hall, which can be used for drill and assembling.

---

[1] These conditions must be satisfied as a condition of the continued recognition of premises approved before the 26th February, 1900, as suitable for day schools or classes for defective children.

(e) Each child must, as a rule, be provided with a single desk of suitable size, and sloped at an angle of from ten to fifteen degrees

(f) The playgrounds must have an area of not less than thirty square feet per child.

(g) There should be a room for the use of the teacher and for the examination of the children by the Medical Officer.

The Playground

There are many schools in England without playgrounds.

The Board of Education now wisely demands that every newly planned school shall have an " open airy playground," proportioned to its size and needs All playgrounds should have a sunny aspect, approximate the square in form, be enclosed, levelled and drained, and be as far as possible free from dangerous corners and buttresses A part of the playground should be covered so as to afford protection from rain. An infants' playground must always be on the same level as the school

Roof playgrounds for senior boys or girls are found here and there in large urban centres Many schools in New York and other large American cities are without playgrounds where they do exist, however, organised effort is made in the States to keep the children from the streets and to interest them in games supervised by teachers and voluntary workers In Berlin and Charlottenburg[1] there is similar enterprise. There, in the summer months, games are organised twice a week from 4 to 6 p m in play and recreation grounds An experiment, too, in providing a course of games during the summer holidays, under various superintendents, has proved exceedingly

[1] See Report of Mr G Andrew to the Scotch Education Department, 1901.

popular—an occasional excursion to places of interest giving to these courses an added charm. Winter, too, has not been left without its organised recreation; for parts of the recreation grounds have been converted into skating rinks, upon which the children, boys at one time and girls at another, have been able to disport themselves.

Similar private effort is in operation in London and some other large English towns, the object being at stated times and at particular centres to teach the children the ideals of play under able superintendents. As an arena for moral training the playground has no rival, for there the social instinct is dominant and ready to put forth those fine qualities associated with it in its best form. Cheerfulness, resource, prudence, justice, sacrifice, delight in the pleasure of others, and the satisfaction that activity gives are taught, cultivated, or strengthened by play under proper conditions.

The playground affords one of the best of opportunities for the teacher to study the characters of the scholars. It is important, therefore, that he should consider his presence there as essential at all reasonable times. Knowledge is always power, and the kind of knowledge that can be acquired in this way is the key to sound progress and the moral betterment of every scholar in the school. Good and bad traits of character exhibited in the playground the teacher can utilise as an object-lesson in the class-room later, and especially employ them to illustrate his weekly hall address.

As play is instinctive, Nature intends it to serve useful ends. For very young children it is the most important of all means of learning. It is the chief agency in development at this period of life; it is the resultant of forces that infants are powerless to resist. The sum of a teacher's efforts as revealed by effects in the process of education is, except in the direction of moral training, almost infinitesimal compared with the knowledge a child acquires through the instruction of Nature's teachers, play and necessity.

With infants, therefore, up to about five years of age, the playground should be, in spirit, the school, and the class-room the accessory. Up to that age rapid growth and development demand a freedom of movement and excite a desire for activity, to which children naturally crave to respond. The variety of employment such as play gives is no doubt the right response to nature's call. The firmer kind of discipline can step in later to correct, enlarge, and round off play and necessity's handiwork.

In summer every opportunity should be seized to utilise the infants' playground for games and other kindergarten instruction. In the words of Pestalozzi, "Neither book nor any product of human skill, but life itself, yields the basis for all education." Again, Wordsworth says, "Dumb yearnings, hidden appetites are ours; and they must have their food." "Come into the light of things, let Nature be your teacher."

"The essential things in education are intellectual interest, freshness of teaching, human sympathy, devotion to high aims. These are spiritual things, and the spirit, like the wind, bloweth where it listeth."[1]

The teacher ought, therefore, to enter upon his work with the spirit of an artist. He should be led, as it were, by that spirit into the schoolroom, where, with the aid of discipline framed on wisdom's firm lines, but softened by sympathy and tempered by genial moral warmth, he will endeavour to mould into the fullest life the plastic materials committed to his keeping.

[1] Mr. Michael E. Sadler, Special Reports, Vol. 9.

INDEX.

219

222

PRINTED AT THE BURLINGTON PRESS, CAMBRIDGE.

BIBLIOLIFE

Old Books Deserve a New Life
www.bibliolife.com

Did you know that you can get most of our titles in our trademark **EasyScript**™ print format? **EasyScript**™ provides readers with a larger than average typeface, for a reading experience that's easier on the eyes.

Did you know that we have an ever-growing collection of books in many languages?

Order online:
www.bibliolife.com/store

Or to exclusively browse our **EasyScript**™ collection:
www.bibliogrande.com

At BiblioLife, we aim to make knowledge more accessible by making thousands of titles available to you – quickly and affordably.

Contact us:
BiblioLife
PO Box 21206
Charleston, SC 29413

1228538R0

Printed in Great Britain by
Amazon.co.uk, Ltd.,
Marston Gate.